HEA

Higher Education Authority
An tÚdarás um Ard-Oideachas

The Higher Education Authority

An tÚdarás um Ard-Oideachas

Marine House, Clanwilliam Court, Dublin 2

Strategy Statement 2004-2007

ISBN 0-904556-80-8

Dublin

Published by The Higher Education Authority

To be purchased from the
Government Publications Sales Office,
Molesworth Street, Dublin 2.

or through any Bookseller

Price €10
2004

OPUB
HEA

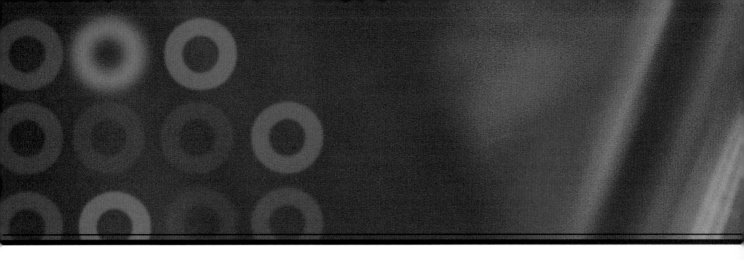

Mission Statement

'To foster the development of a higher education sector which is **accessible to all** potential students and which is **recognised internationally** for the **high quality of teaching, learning and research** and which has the capacity to address the changing needs and challenges in our society.'

contents

Chapters

Appendices

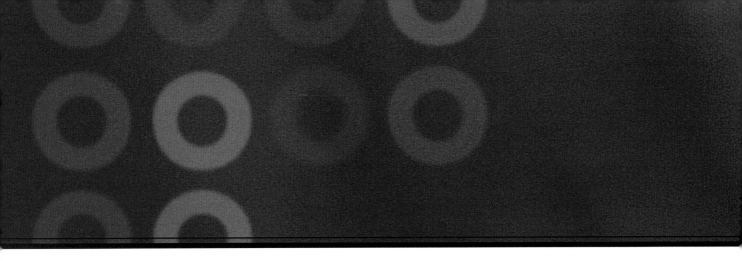

Foreword

Higher education plays a central role in developing and sustaining an advanced society. Participation in higher education supports both personal development and national, social, cultural and economic development. The higher education sector is a vital national resource.

Ireland has made considerable progress economically and socially in recent years. We have done so through a mix of policies, incorporating social partnership, pro-enterprise taxation policies, the attraction of foreign direct investment and technology, and improved systems of public governance and administration. Above all our success has depended upon the provision of a high quality education system, responsive to the needs of individuals, society and the economy.

As well as creating new opportunities, progress has been accompanied by new challenges and problems. Areas of public service provision show strains of historical under-investment - this is particularly true of the health services and the education system. There are also indications of social stress, symptomatic of a society in which not all have benefited, or not to the same extent, and where some are finding it difficult to cope with change.

If Ireland as a society and an economy is to continue to develop, we must urgently adopt the strategies necessary to create a dynamic, knowledge-based, innovative and inclusive society. If we fail to do so then not only will we not develop further but we risk losing the gains from the significant progress that has been made.

In our 2002 strategy document on research, development and innovation - *Creating and Sustaining the Innovation Society* - the Higher Education Authority (HEA) described the necessary transition as being a paradigm shift, such was the change in public policy required to put innovation at the centre of the policy agenda. This includes major actions and strategic investments in what we described as knowledge production and knowledge transfer and development.

The higher education sector has a vital role to play - in educating and in training the knowledge workers of the future; in being the central resource for research, development and innovation; in creating the innovation capacity to develop new businesses, services and products; in cultural development; and in enhancing social cohesion and understanding in our society, not least by improving the level and sophistication of analysis and debate.

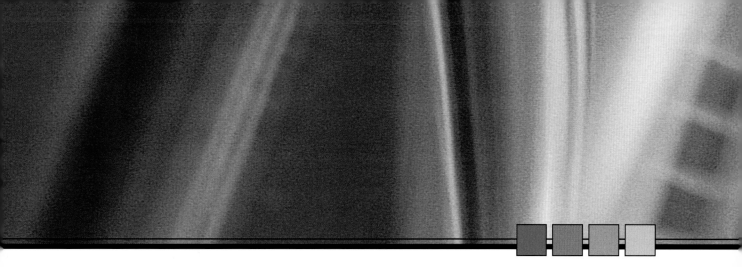

Development of our human resources will be especially critical in meeting the challenges Ireland faces. In the past we have often succeeded by learning from other societies. If we are to be a society at the frontier of development we must rely less on imitation and instead be increasingly innovative and creative. An innovation society needs well-informed people who are creative, questioning, inventive, disciplined and who have good judgement and are capable of responding creatively and constructively to change. The education system, and particularly the higher education sector, have an essential role in creating this quality of human resources.

Although this document sets out the HEA's key strategic objectives for the next three years, it should be regarded as an interim document. A key factor which will influence the execution of this Strategy Statement is the review of higher education which is being carried out by the Organisation for Economic Cooperation and Development (OECD) at the request of the Minister for Education and Science. The HEA welcomes this review and has made a submission to the review team setting out our views and proposals on a wide range of issues including the strategic management and structure of the sector, investment and financing, research and development, teaching and learning. We look forward to the outcome and recommendations of the OECD and in light of Government decisions and actions in response to these recommendations, we will reassess this Strategy Statement and make any appropriate revisions.

In preparing this document, the Authority has consulted with, and taken on board the views of, the stakeholders set out in Appendix 4. The Authority is committed to continuing to work with the stakeholders to achieve our strategic objectives.

Dr Don Thornhill
HEA CHAIRMAN

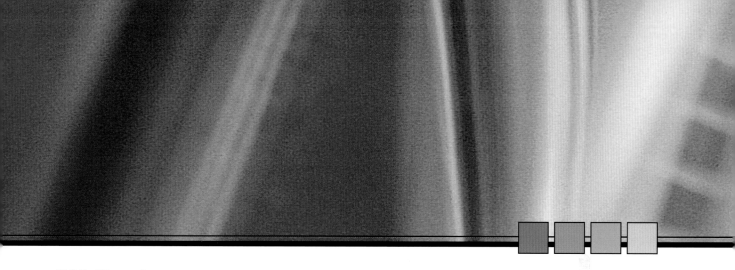

HEA Members

Chairman: Dr. Don Thornhill,
Higher Education Authority.

Professor Tom Boylan
Department of Economics,
National University of Ireland, Galway

Dr. Maurice Bric,
Department of Modern History,
University College Dublin.

Mr. William James Caves,
Former Chief Executive, Northern Ireland Schools
Examinations and Assessment Council (CCEA)

Cllr. Maria Corrigan,
Member Dún Laoghaire Rathdown County Council

Mr. Martin Cronin,
Chief Executive Forfás

Dr. Honor Fagan,
Department of Sociology NUI Maynooth

Ms Maura Grant
Director of Programmes relating to Educational
Disadvantage,
Department of Education and Science

Professor Gary Granville
Faculty of Education,
National College and Art and Design

Ms Carol Marie Herron,
Education Co-ordinator,
Co. Cavan VEC and Cavan Partnership

Mr. Paul Hannigan
Director, Letterkenny Institute of Technology

Mr. Patrick J. Kirby
Group Commercial Director, Alphyra

Ms Monica Leech
Communications Consultant

Professor Tom McCarthy
Professor of Economics and Dean of Business School,
Dublin City University

Ms Antoinette Nic Gearailt
Principal, The Donahies Community School, Dublin 13

Mr. Barry O'Brien,
Director (Estate and Support Services),
Royal College of Surgeons in Ireland

Professor Sarah Moore,
Dean of Teaching and Learning, University of Limerick

Professor Ciaran Murphy,
Department of Accounting ,
Finance & Information Systems,
University College Cork

Mr. Will Priestley,
President, Union of Students in Ireland

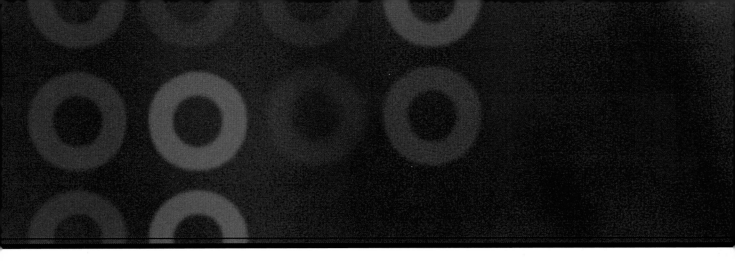

HEA Executive

Secretary/Chief Executive	Tom Boland	**Assistant Secretary**	George Ryan
			Physical Development
Deputy Chief Executive	Mary Kerr		
		Senior Policy Analyst	Orla Christle
Head of Policy and Planning	Fergal Costello		*National Office for Equity of*
			Access to Higher Education
Head of Research Programmes	Dr. Eucharia Meehan		
		Programme Manager	Peter Brown
Head of National Office	Dr. Mary-Liz Trant		*National Office for Equity of*
for Equity of Access			*Access to Higher Education*
to Higher Education			
		Senior Policy Analyst	Caitriona Ryan
Head of Administration	Padraic Mellett		*Policy and Planning*
Head of Information	Gerry O'Sullivan	**Recurrent Grants**	Jane Sweetman
And Public Affairs			Mary May
			Valerie Harvey
Head of ICT Skills Programme	Pat O'Connor	**Industrial Relations Unit**	Maura O'Shea
			Justin Sinnott
Management Accountant	Stewart Roche		
		Physical Development	Ciaran Dolan
Assistant Secretary	Mary Armstrong		Patricia Carroll
	Recurrent Grants		Brendan Ferron
Assistant Secretary	Sheena Duffy	**European Programmes**	Louise Sherry
	Research, Socrates/Erasmus		Adrian O'Donoghue
Assistant Secretary	Jennifer Gygax	**Policy And Planning**	Leonora Harty
	Recurrent Grants		Rowena Dwyer

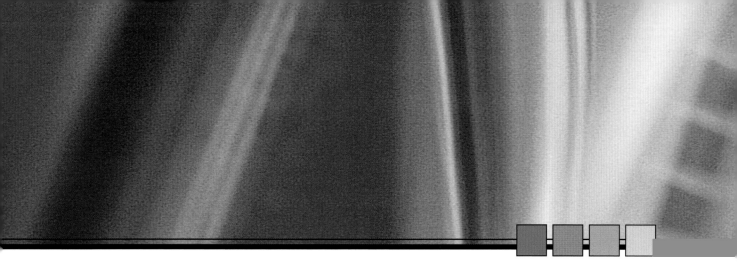

HEA Executive

Statistics Section	Barbara Carr	**Secretarial Services**	Jacintha Healy
	Oliver Mooney		*(Secretary to Chairman)*
	Frank Condon		Mary Dunne
			(Secretary to Chief Executive)
Research Programmes	Dr. Lisa Higgins		Mary Meade
	Fiona Davis		Kate Philbin-Dargan
	Dr. Emer Cunningham		
	Eileen O'Connell		
	Adrian O'Donoghue	**Reception**	Shauna Brennan
			(Marine House)
National Office for Equity of	Olive Walsh		Graham Barry
Access to Higher Education	Alan McGrath		*(Brooklawn House)*
	Brian Johnston		
	Justin Synnott	**Services**	Bridget Kelly
	Modesta Mawarire		Caroline Curtis
Information and Public Affairs	Cliona Buckley		
Personnel and Accounts	Niall O'Connell		
	Emer McMullin		
	Sharon O'Rourke		
Information Technology	John Muldoon		
	(IT Manager)		
	Marie O'Sullivan		
	(Network Administrator)		

introduction

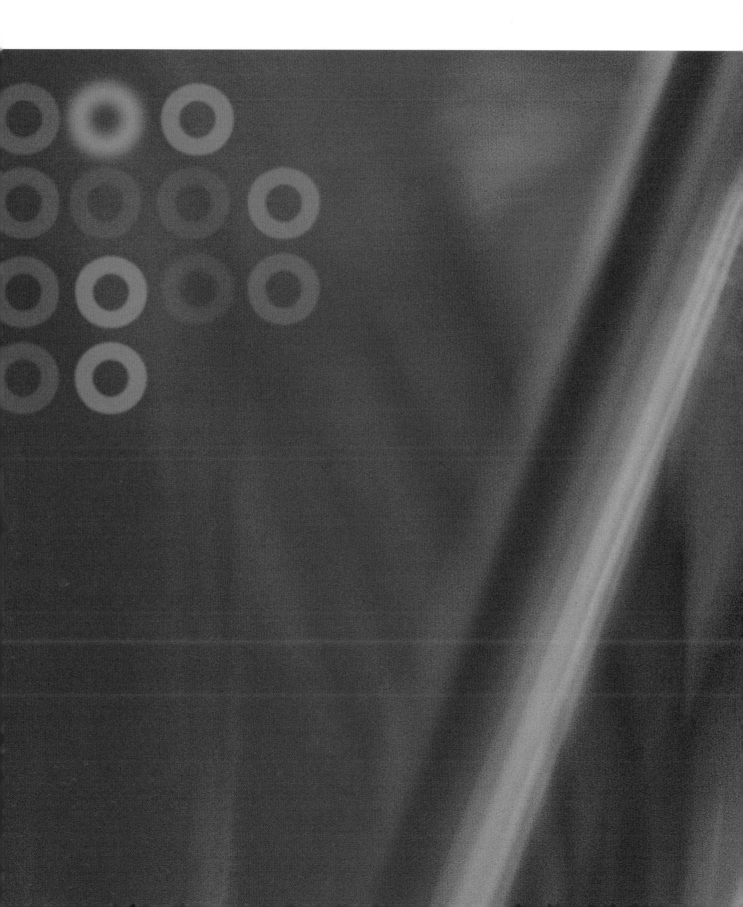

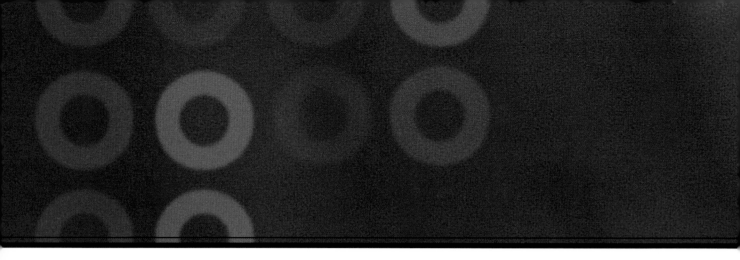

Introduction

The HEA

The Higher Education Authority (HEA) is a statutory body[1]. We advise Government on the development of higher education and research in Ireland. The HEA is also responsible for the funding of the universities and other institutions designated under the Higher Education Authority Act 1971, and for the management of the Programme for Research in Third Level Institutions (PRTLI). The Government has also signalled its intention to transfer responsibility for Exchequer funding of the institutes of technology to the HEA.

The HEA has a transcending role in fostering the development of a higher education sector that can collectively support national development in all its dimensions, economic social and cultural. We do this through supporting the public and statutory institutions involved in higher education and research. We provide that support through -

- developing and publishing relevant policy, strategy and priorities

- advising the higher education institutions in their development

- funding the institutions in their provision of higher education and research programmes.

Our Responsibilities to Stakeholders

As a statutory body charged with a range of specific functions, we have a responsibility to the Minister and Department of Education and Science and, through them, to the Government, the Oireachtas and society, to ensure that we carry out our funding activities properly and efficiently, in accordance with public policy and the rules and procedures for the public finances.

Our responsibilities to Ministers, to their Departments, to Government and to the Oireachtas also extend to our policy advice. Our policy advice, and recommendations will always be informed by our objective assessment and evaluation of the needs of Irish society and of the optimum strategies for addressing them.

---

1 The HEA was set up initially on an ad hoc basis in 1968, and was given statutory powers in the Higher Education Authority Act, 1971. Some of the key contributions of the HEA to higher education over the last number of years are set out in appendix 3.

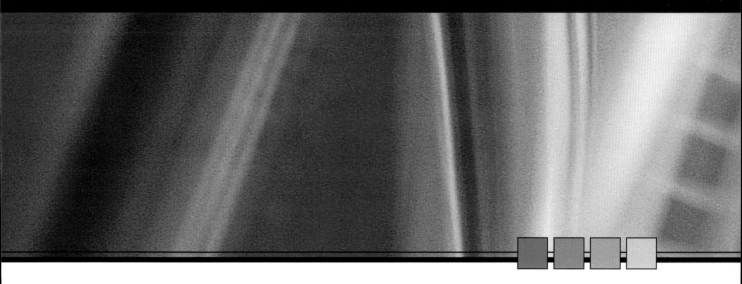

We have a particular responsibility to inform ourselves of the views of those actively involved in the higher education sector, including the perspectives, needs and challenges faced by students and the academic communities. We see it as essential that all stakeholders recognise our objectivity, but also our insight and understanding of their viewpoints and concerns, without prejudice to our obligations to act and advise in the national interest in accordance with our statutory obligations.

Operating Principles

Our operating principles include the following:

- A commitment to a higher education and research sector of the highest quality and accessibility.

- Supporting the institutions in their missions to provide students with the opportunity to fully participate in, and benefit from, higher education.

- Ensuring that the core recurrent funding of third level institutions is allocated in a way which is equitable and transparent.

- Ensuring that incremental strategic recurrent financing is distributed on the basis of transparent, criteria-based competitive processes.

- To have increasing recourse to criteria based allocation processes (including competition) for major initiatives in capital spending and in research expenditure.

- To ensure that appropriate accountability frameworks and arrangements are in place in respect of the significant Exchequer investment in higher education.

- To ensure that all stakeholders, particularly the public and Government and the Oireachtas, have confidence in the management of the sector and of its institutions.

chapter one | The Operational Environment

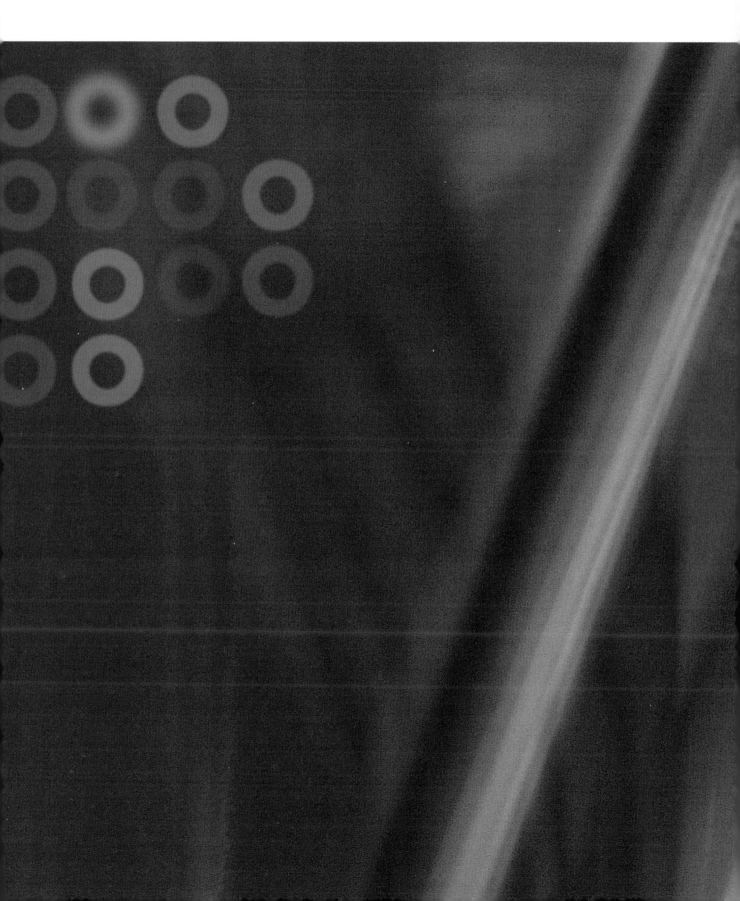

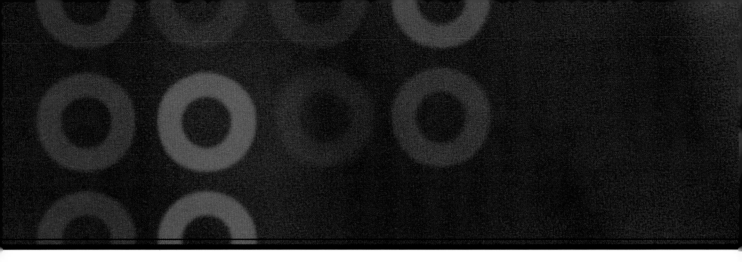

1. The Operational Environment

This strategy has been prepared in the context of a rapidly changing national and international environment. In particular, two important challenges have influenced the strategies and objectives set out in this document. These are:

- Increasing participation in higher education
- Creating and sustaining an innovation society

Increasing participation in higher education

When the HEA was established more than thirty years ago the proportion of school-leavers entering higher education was about 10%[2]. Now it is approximately 56%[3]. The policy objective pursued by successive Governments of increasing participation in higher education has been remarkably successful. The complex challenges and needs of a modern society are likely to require further increases in the overall participation rate. It is important to support further access to higher education so that all citizens have the opportunity to develop to their full potential. There is a particular need to promote access to third level education for students with a disability and students with economic, social and other disadvantages. There is also a need to provide opportunities to those who could not participate when leaving school or whose career and personal development would be enhanced by a return to higher education. The institutions will need to respond to these and other evolving needs through an increasing diversity in programmes, curriculum, course structures and timetables.The sector has an important role to play in giving substance to the concept of life long learning.

The processes of teaching and learning are also evolving. 'Distance' and outreach education can make higher education more accessible. The advent of e-learning, both as a vehicle for distance education and also for enhancing teaching and learning within institutions, offers new opportunities and challenges and in particular has prompted the entry into the sector of new providers of higher education.

These changes and demands are occurring at a time when the number of school leavers is falling, after a long period of sustained growth. For most of the last twenty years the demand for higher education from school leavers exceeded the number of places available. While we expect continuing growth in demand for higher education places,

---

2 Source: Interim Report of the Technical Working Group of the Steering Committee on the Future Development of Higher Education, January 1995 (based on OECD data) – refers to year 1965.

3 Source: Department of Education and Science.

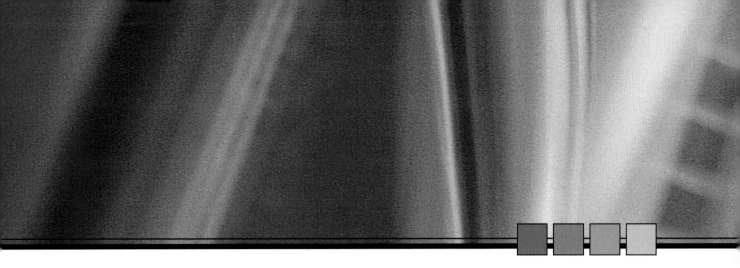

the sources of growth are likely to change, with greater demands from mature students and other underrepresented groups. These changes provide both an incentive and a challenge for institutions. Competition between institutions for students is likely but there will also be opportunities to respond to new needs and challenges. There are also opportunities to promote Ireland as a destination for overseas students[4].

Creating and sustaining an innovation society

Higher education has an essential role to play in enhancing the education levels of the population and particularly of the labour force - and thereby contributing to economic and social development. The environment in which the institutions are expected to meet these demands is becoming increasingly complex and demanding. The pace of change is quickening and the expectations of Government and society are increasing. The HEA has argued in our research strategy policy document, *Creating and Sustaining the Innovation Society*[5], that future economic development strategy can no longer afford to rely on the application of knowledge generated in other countries and that a transformation to an innovation society is essential if Ireland is to secure its position as a prosperous and socially advanced society. Furthermore, Ireland is committed to the "Lisbon" target of the EU to achieve a 3% level of GERD (general expenditure on R&D as a percentage of GDP) by 2010.

Innovation is the successful application for development - particularly in the business sector - of new knowledge. Research is the source of new knowledge.

The higher education institutions, and particularly the universities and institutes of technology, have an essential part to play in this major national undertaking. They need, increasingly, to become the sources of new knowledge through research and the means for its application through applied research, through development and through the commercialisation of research by the sale and licensing of intellectual property and through involvement in the creation of new 'spin-off' companies.

---

4 The Minister for Education and Science has established an inter-departmental committee to consider this issue. The HEA has published a policy document – *Provision of Undergraduate and Taught Postgraduate Education to Overseas Students in Ireland (August 2003).*

5 *Creating and Sustaining the Innovation Society,* Higher Education Authority, July 2002

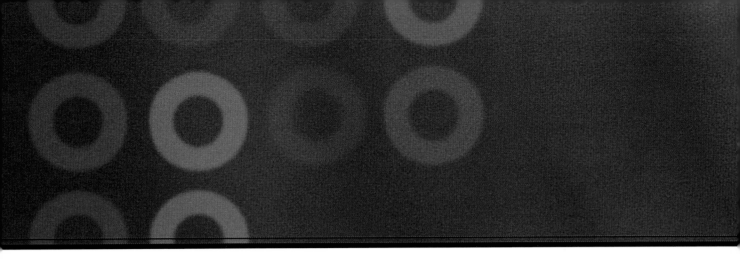

In the National Development Plan for 2000-2006, the Government allocated €2.471bn for research, technological development and innovation. Much of this allocation is being directed at funding research in the higher education sector. The HEA is managing the Programme for Research in Third Level Institutions (PRTLI) on behalf of the Minister for Education and Science. €605m has been allocated by the HEA to support the strategic development of the research activities of the third level institutions[6]. The Government has also established Science Foundation Ireland (SFI) with a mandate and a budget of over €700m to support research in the strategically important areas of biotechnology and information and communications technologies. Research programmes and activities funded by SFI are now being undertaken in the third level sector as are research programmes funded by other organisations including Enterprise Ireland and the Health Research Board (see appendix 2 for graphical illustration of research infrastructure).

This new role for higher education institutions, as 'engines' of economic growth and development, poses new challenges and opportunities. Responding to these challenges will require higher levels of funding. It is unlikely, given other demands, that all additional funding needs can be provided by the Exchequer. Currently, the university sector receives over 80% of its income from public sector sources (the figure is over 90% for the institute of technology sector). Accordingly, we see an increased future role for private funding (e.g. tuition fees, research, contract and investment income, income from commercial services such as canteens, shops, etc. and income from technology transfer and commercialisation of intellectual property) and we will encourage the institutions in their efforts to broaden and diversify their funding sources.

Creating a positive environment - the role of the HEA

The higher education system competes for resources nationally and internationally. It cannot be taken for granted that, in an increasingly competitive environment, with continued pressure on the public finances, the case for investing in higher education and research will be unanimously accepted. It is essential that an explicit, proactive effort be made to ensure that the wider environment in which higher education operates is conducive to the maintenance and further enhancement of a vibrant and dynamic higher education and research system. The substantive work to be done in this regard by the HEA includes:

---

6 The successful impact of PRTLI have been noted in our recent publication - *The PRTLI Transforming the Irish Research in Education Landscape* (2003)

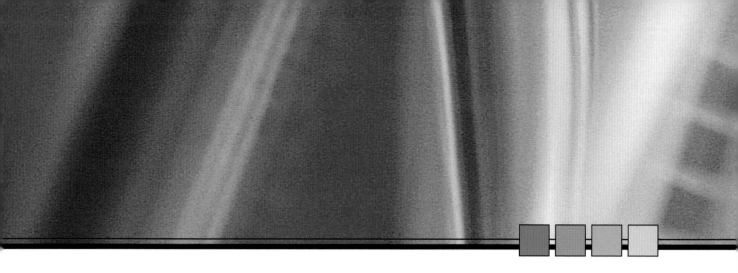

- Building an understanding among all constituencies of the role and critical importance of higher education and research and specifically of the close connection between teaching, learning and research.

- Promoting growth in investment in basic research and increased commercialisation and application of the results from the research for economic and social development.

- Supporting the higher education institutions in developing, sustaining and in positioning the research system in Ireland.

- Supporting the higher education institutions in their plans for development, within a framework of meaningful accountability, value for money and support for national needs.

- Constructing the case for, and seeking to secure, necessary financial resources for the sector.

- Advising on the updating, when needed, of the legislative framework within which the institutions in the sector operate.

- Creating a context conducive to healthy differentiation and specialisation within the sector, with competition and collaboration as appropriate among institutions in the interest of achieving efficiencies, economies of scale and critical mass across the sector.

- Developing effective relationships and partnerships with the other major stakeholders in higher education. These are primarily the institutions themselves, students, the Department of Education and Science, other Government Departments, particularly the Departments of Enterprise Trade and Employment, Finance and Health and Children, the Research Councils, the Health Research Board, Science Foundation Ireland, the National Qualifications Authority of Ireland, the Higher Education and Training Awards Council, the Further Education and Training Awards Council, the Irish Business and Employers Confederation and the Irish Congress of Trade Unions, and appropriate policy advisory bodies such as Forfás, Enterprise Ireland and IDA Ireland.

chapter two | Mission and Strategic Priorities

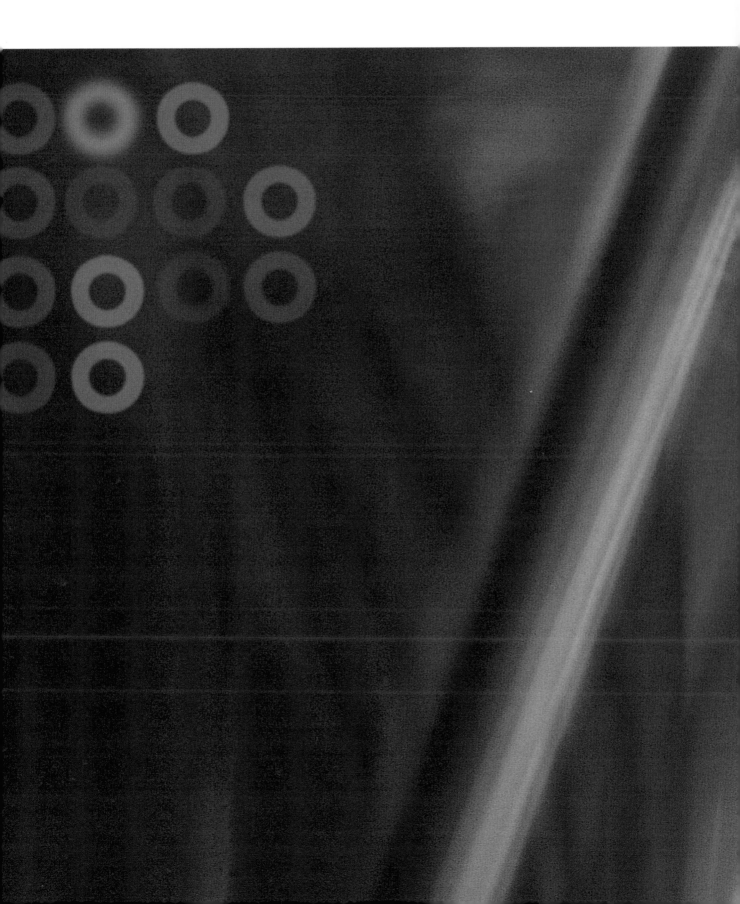

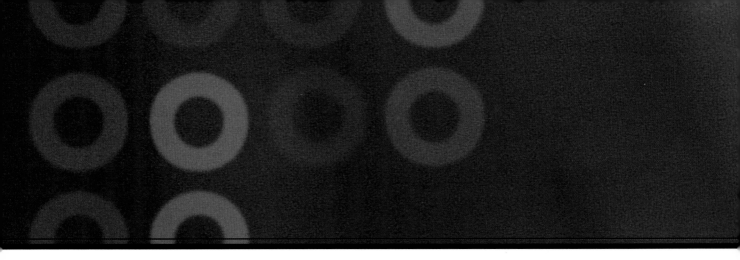

2. Mission and Strategic Priorities

The HEA Mission is: -

'To foster the development of a higher education sector which is **accessible to all** potential students, which is **recognised internationally** for the **high quality of teaching, learning and research** and which has the capacity to address the changing needs and challenges in our society.'

Critical Target

In order to assess progress and achievements towards the realisation of this mission the Authority has set as its overarching critical target that:

*The higher education sector in Ireland should be at or above the **top quartile of OECD countries** in terms of both graduation rates and funding levels. Working with the Department of Education and Science and other stakeholders, the objective is that as a first step this position be reached by the end of the period of this strategy statement. This in itself is not sufficient. Ireland is committed as part of the Lisbon Strategy of making the EU the world's most dynamic, competitive and sustainable knowledge based economy. As part of that objective, world class performance in higher education and research is required. Accordingly we set as our overarching aim that Ireland's higher education sector will be within the **first decile of OECD higher education systems** by 2010.*

Based on most recent figures[7] Ireland is in the top quartile only in respect of graduation rates at Diploma/Certificate (2nd of 15 countries surveyed). In the case of graduation rates at Degree and Advanced Research Degree levels, Ireland is ranked 11th (of 17 countries) and 14th (of 27 countries) respectively.

Analysis of Ireland's positioning with respect to funding levels is a complex task. It must take into account both our total allocation of resources to higher education and research as a percentage of national income and also the size of our student population.

---

7 Source: Education at a Glance, OECD Indicators (2003). The year of reference for graduation indicators is 2001; for expenditure figures it is 2000.

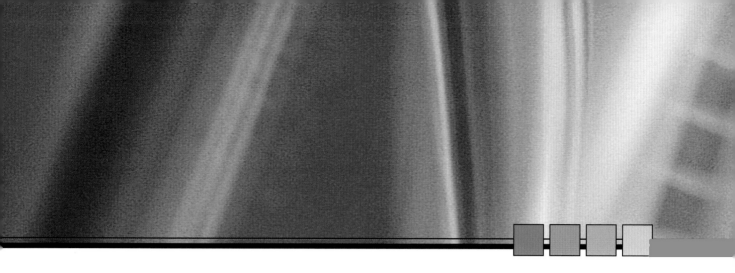

Expenditure on higher education institutions as a percentage of GDP in 2000 was 1.6%, ranking us 8th out of 29 countries surveyed. However, there is ongoing debate regarding the appropriateness of using a GDP indicator or a GNP/GNI indicator given the size of our net outgoing national factor income from abroad. Therefore, a better and more reliable indicator is to review the level of expenditure on tertiary education institutions expressed on a per student basis. This indicates that Ireland in 2000 was positioned outside of the top quartile of OECD countries, at 9th place of 28 countries.

These figures demonstrate that Ireland has not achieved the "top quartile" strategic target for performance in higher education.

Strategic Priorities

This strategy statement will inform our operations and business planning over the next three years. Our strategic priorities are now outlined, along with key areas for action. In preparing the strategy statement the Authority has taken into account:

- the statutory duties of the Authority as set out in the Higher Education Act, 1971, the Universities Act, 1997 and the Qualifications (Education and Training) Act, 1999
- Government policies as set out in the *Programme for a New Millennium*
- the challenges for the development of the higher education sector in Ireland.

The following are our strategic priorities:
1. Empower the institutions - to develop the highest quality of teaching, learning, scholarship and research and enhance their contribution to society and to economic development.
2. Widen participation in higher education.
3. Foster the development of a higher education sector which has the capacity to respond to changing needs in society.
4. Strengthen the organisational capability of the HEA itself.

The first three core strategies underpin the key areas for action identified by the Authority for the coming three years, as set out in this strategy statement. To enable the HEA to achieve these strategies, the fourth strategy addresses the development of the HEA itself.

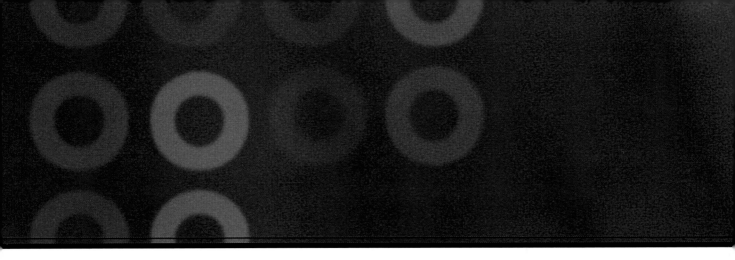

OECD Review

A major factor which will influence the execution of this Strategy Statement is the review of higher education which is being carried out by the Organisation for Economic Cooperation and Development (OECD) at the request of the Minister for Education and Science, e.g. an issue which the OECD is likely to consider is the process for the transfer of exchequer funding responsibilities for the institute of technology sector from the Department of Education and Science to the HEA. The HEA welcomes this review and will assist in every way we can. We look forward to its outcome and recommendations. In light of Government decisions and actions in response to the recommendations of the OECD, we will reassess this Strategy Statement.

Overview of Key Objectives

The following paragraphs provide an overview of the key objectives behind each of our strategic priorities.

(1) Empowering the Institutions

The institutions in the third level sector - universities, institutes of technology, colleges of education and other colleges - are the key means of ensuring that Irish higher education achieves a top ranking position in the OECD. The HEA is not a direct provider of higher education. Its key strategic priority is to support the institutions to be recognised internationally for the high quality of teaching, learning, research and innovation and in doing so to address the needs and challenges faced by Irish society. The institutions must also demonstrate value for money and effectiveness and be accountable to the public in their use of public funds in achieving their objectives.

The HEA welcomes proposals to transfer responsibility for the Exchequer funding of the institutes of technology from the Department of Education and Science to the HEA. The institutes of technology have contributed very significantly to higher education in Ireland and to economic and social development. The HEA looks forward to working more closely with the institutes on the basis of increased institutional autonomy and enhanced accountability.

(2) Widening participation in higher education

A key concern for higher education today, is the need to support all potential students to access higher education. Access to higher education provides for enhanced life opportunities. Increasing participation in higher education

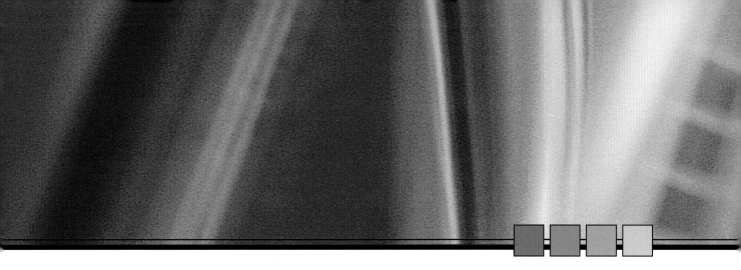

supports enhanced social inclusion and economic and cultural development. Accordingly, an overarching strategic objective for the HEA is to foster the development of a higher education sector which is accessible to all potential students.

(3) Fostering the development of a higher education sector which has the capacity to respond to changing needs in society

The core role of higher education has always been the generation, dissemination and exploitation of new knowledge. The higher education sector must also have regard to the changing needs of the society in which it is located. Accordingly, a key strategic objective for the HEA will be to foster the development of a higher education sector which has the capability to respond to changing needs in society.

(4) Strengthening HEA capability

The HEA recognises that its staff are its most valuable resource and central to the successful delivery of this strategy. The HEA supports an on-going process of staff development and is committed to the provision of training and development opportunities. It will also work to ensure that internal structures and procedures facilitate maximum efficiencies. The performance of the organisation will be continually reviewed.

The table overleaf sets out the four strategic priorities and the key areas for action that have been identified for each priority over the timeframe of this strategy. This statement then goes on to elaborate more fully on each of the key actions.

Strategic Priorities

Empowering the institutions	Widening participation in higher education	Fostering the development of a higher education sector which has the capacity to respond to changing needs in society	Strengthening HEA capability
Key areas for action	**Key areas for action**	**Key areas for action**	**Key areas for action**
Put in place **funding frameworks and instruments** which support the institutions in achieving **excellence in teaching, learning, research** and services to society.	Promote **equity of access and opportunity** in higher education.	**Advise** the Minister for Education and Science and Government on all matters pertaining to higher education and assuring Government and the general public as to the effectiveness and efficiency of the system.	**Maintain** appropriate resources and skill sets **to meet expanding needs.**
Support the development of **research infrastructure** to meet national research priorities.	**Promote successful participation** in higher education.	Develop policies and procedures to ensure that the Irish system is **appropriately linked to European** and wider international systems of higher education.	Introduce and continually upgrade **quality** and **performance management systems.**
Fostering the disciplines of **strategic management** and associated organisational change and **capacity building among the institutions** that comprise the sector.	Foster links that facilitate **student movement and progression** within the education system as a whole.	**Monitor developments** on a global stage and locally that are relevant to higher education in Ireland.	Invest and upgrade the physical resources, (premises, IT systems) required to carry out organisational functions and objectives.
Foster the development as appropriate, of comprehensive systems of **evaluation** which provide the basis of good governance and accountability; the stimulus to innovative, progressive action to enhance quality and breadth of provision to diverse participants; and the means for benchmarking against international standards.		Contribute and support other agencies / bodies in the development of policy.	

chapter three | Strategic Priorities - Key Actions

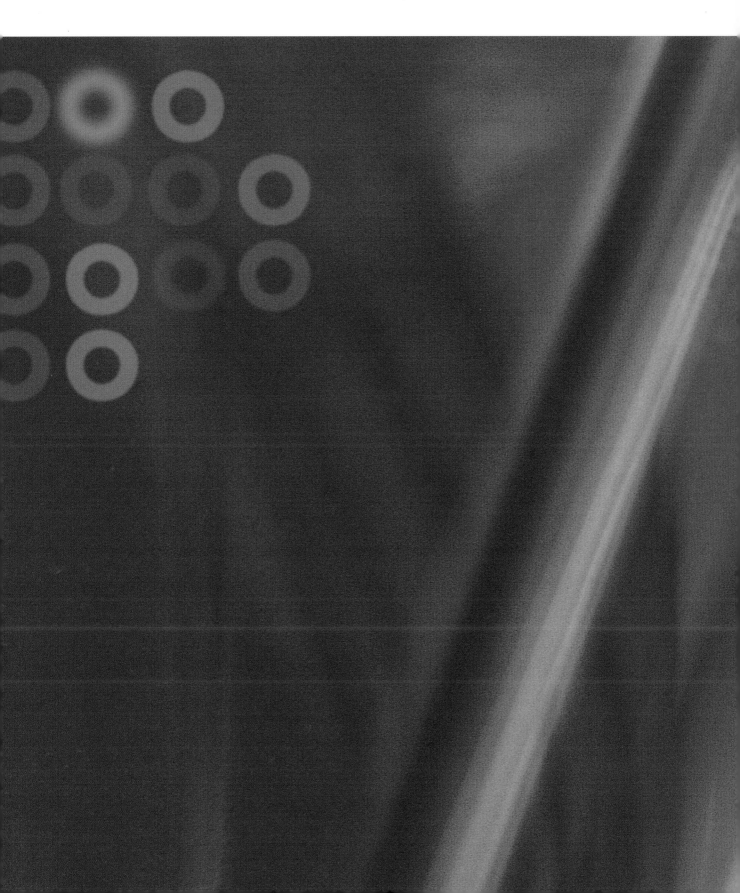

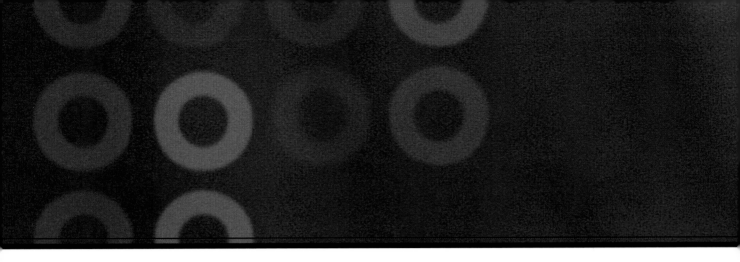

3. Strategic Priorities - Key Actions

This section identifies at a high level some of the key actions necessary to contribute to the achievement of the strategic priorities. The actions identified are not necessarily exhaustive, but give an indication of the work which the Authority intends to carry out over 2004/2007 to achieve our strategic priorities.

An important point to note is that some of the key actions set out below will contribute to a number of objectives. It should be noted, for example, that the development of the model for the recurrent funding will have a role in supporting enhanced access, participation, and progression as well as supporting the development of institutional strategies and capability. Similarly, the initiation of the joint HEA/IUQB review of the quality assurance procedures in the universities should not only contribute to empowering the universities, but also to promoting access and to the wider development of the higher education sector. For ease of reference therefore, key actions are presented in the area of most immediate relevance.

It should also be noted that the range of activities and outputs of the HEA are greater than those described in the following pages. For example, the assessment of the funding requirements and proposals of the designated institutions is a continuing and vital part of the activity of the HEA which requires continuing contact with the institutions and with Government departments, particularly the Department of Education and Science; the Authority is continually involved in monitoring and reviewing the financial position of institutions. The HEA will carry out this and other tasks in accordance with our strategic priorities.

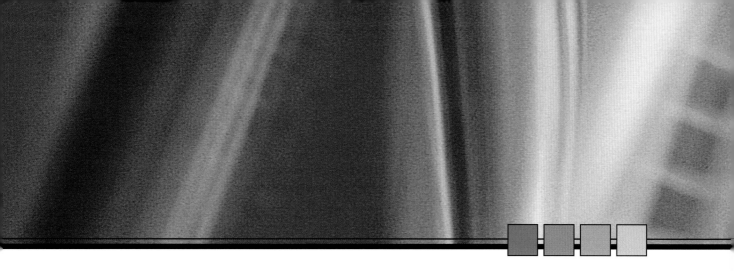

(1) Empowering Institutions

> **Key area for action**
>
> *Put in place funding frameworks and instruments that support the institutions in achieving excellence in teaching, learning, research and services to society and which enhance their accountability for the expenditure of public funds. Particular attention will be paid to developing a policy framework which facilitates the higher education institutions to increase revenues from non-Exchequer sources and to develop internal strategic independence and autonomy.*

Key Tasks

Review and report on the procedures for quality assurance in the universities

The universities have a statutory function to develop and implement quality assurance procedures aimed at improving the quality of educational and other services provided by the university. The HEA together with the Irish Universities Quality Board (IUQB) have initiated the first external review of such procedures. The review will be undertaken by distinguished international experts and will support the universities in ensuring the best quality in the provision of their services, as well as meeting accountability requirements. The report of the review will be available by end 2004.

Review of Recurrent Funding Model

The HEA is reviewing the funding allocation system for higher education institutions. The review is wide-ranging in scope and will explore potential approaches to the future resourcing and support of the higher education institutions that can best enable achievement of the strategic objectives of the sector including the principles of academic freedom and institutional autonomy. The recurrent funding model is also the key mechanism through which accountability can be ensured. The review is being undertaken in the context of the challenges facing higher education, for example, -

- broadening access to higher education, particularly access by mature students and those from disadvantaged socio-economic backgrounds;
- growing concern with issues such as quality, relevance and value for money;

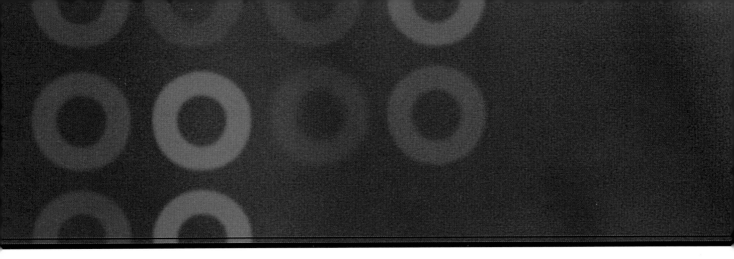

- the need to respond to growing public policy emphasis on research and development;

- the growing need for institutions to develop a diversity of funding sources.

A consultation paper has been prepared in spring 2004 and, following agreement, implementation of the new model will proceed.

To review and prioritise all future capital projects

The HEA has been requested by the Minister for Education and Science to undertake a review exercise of all capital projects in the third level sector, already submitted or which institutions intend to submit. This is with a view to prioritisation and phasing in the context of a multi-annual programme. This review is being undertaken against a background of very considerable demands on the Exchequer for capital financing, as well as the limited availability of capital funding from the Exchequer across all areas of Government expenditure. A working group has been established to conduct the prioritisation exercise, and submit a schedule of projects, with recommendations, for consideration by the Authority. The Authority will subsequently make recommendations to the Minister in summer 2004.

To develop a new model for the management of the HEA capital programme

A new set of procedures for the implementation and management of the HEA Capital Programme is being developed, in conjunction with the Department of Education and Science. The objective is to introduce a devolved scheme, transferring greater autonomy and responsibility to the institutions, thus allowing all future capital projects to be progressed in a more efficient and cost-effective manner. Proposals for a new model will be developed and submitted to the Minister in 2004. Agreed changes to the model will be implemented by the Authority.

To address identified skills needs

The HEA will work with other government departments, bodies, agencies and the higher education institutions in the area of identifying and addressing skills needs. The HEA will put in place funding frameworks that support the institutions to develop educational programmes that meet skills needs. A recent example is the Information Technology Investment Fund in 2001 which was established to support the provision of high-level IT courses by third level institutions.

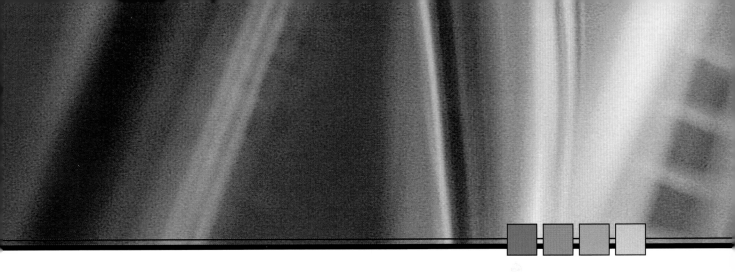

Key Outputs 2004 - 2007
Support institutions in achieving excellence in teaching, learning and research

1. Report: *University Quality Assurance (QA) Procedures* (2004)

2. Report: *Review of Recurrent Funding Model* (2004)

3. Report: *Capital Prioritisation Review Group* (2004)

4. Development of proposals for a new model of capital programme management (2004)

5. Development and implementation of funding frameworks to support skills needs, as appropriate - management of the Investment Technology Investment Fund (on-going)

Key area for action
Support the development of research infrastructure to meet national research priorities.

Key Tasks

Evaluate the impact of the PRTLI on research policy, quality of research and training and learning in the institutions

Unprecedented levels of funding have been provided through the PRTLI to support the development of research capacity in the higher education sector. The programme has to date allocated some €600 million to support research programmes. The impact of this funding on the higher education sector will be evaluated. The report of the impact assessment will be completed in summer 2004.

Determine strategic direction and contribute to the next national development plan

Arising from the PRTLI impact assessment, we will consider the best approach to the future strategic direction of research funding and PRTLI and contribute to the development of the next national development plan in 2005/2006.

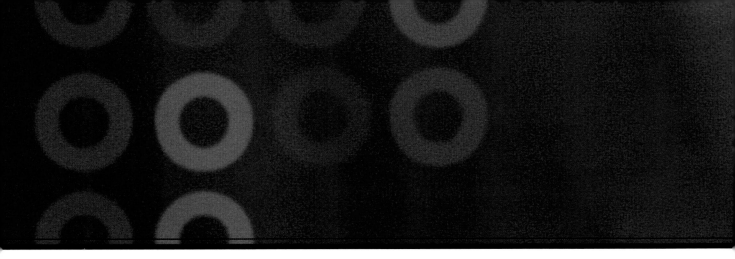

Allocation of PRTLI funding (Cycle 4) as approved under the National Development Plan (NDP)

The PRTLI has had a critical role in developing the research base within the higher education institutions. It has contributed to institutions adopting a broad strategic approach to research as well as a willingness to collaborate with others in joint initiatives to develop their research strategies. It is essential that this investment should continue. The PRTLI impact assessment and policy review (which is a key component of the impact assessment) will inform the parameters and criteria for PRTLI Cycle 4. It is expected that the call for proposals under PRTLI Cycle 4 will take place before the end of 2004 and the allocations will be made in 2005.

Support the higher education institutions in attracting and retaining researchers, to support the development of a durable national research capacity

The HEA has together with Forfás and other stakeholders, undertaken a review of strategies and systems to attract and retain researchers in Irish higher education[8]. The report sets out a series of recommendations that the HEA and other concerned stakeholders will work to address into the future. Specific recommendations include actions aimed at improving career structures for professional researchers and developing international research manpower programmes to attract postgraduates, post-doctorates and principal investigators.

To support the HEIs in exploiting the opportunities presented by the European Research Area (ERA)

The HEA has established its own expert group which will engage with a range of key stakeholders (e.g. Department of Enterprise, Trade and Employment) to plan for, and to advise on, the development of the ERA. The HEA is committed to supporting the institutions to flourish in a Europe of knowledge.

---

8   Report: Creating Ireland's Innovation Society: The Next Strategic Step - Attracting and Retaining World Class Researchers (2003)

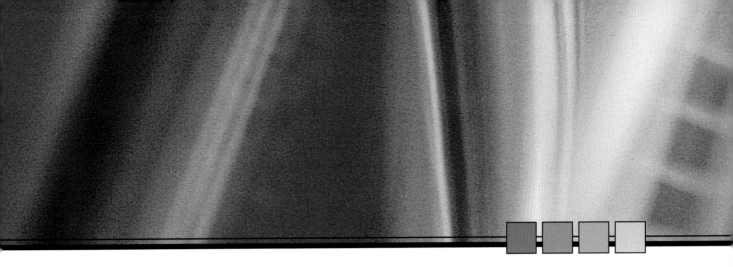

To support the management of research funding

Through the Standing Committee of Research Funding Agencies (Merrion Group)[9] the HEA will work with other research funding bodies in order to support a coherent approach to the management of research funding so as to maximise operational efficiencies and minimise the administrative burden on researchers. The Merrion objectives encourage collaboration among agencies in the research area for the purposes of enhancing the research system as a whole.

Key Outputs 2004 - 2007
Support the development of research infrastructure to meet national research priorities

1. Report: *Impact Assessment of PRTLI* (2004)

2. Contributing to the formulation of the next national development plan (2005/2006)

3. Outline structure for parameters and process for PRTLI Cycle 4 allocations (2004/2005)

4. Implementation of a range of measures aimed at attracting and retaining researchers in Ireland (on-going)

5. Provision of advice and support to higher education institutions in relation to the European Research Area (on-going)

6. Support for the management of research funding through the Merrion Group (on-going)

---

9 The "Standing Committee of Research Funding Agencies" (known as the Merrion Group) was established in 2002 when a number of research funding bodies agreed to work together to maximise the contribution of their organisations to achieving the national goal of building world class research capacity in Ireland. A Standing Committee of the research funding bodies was subsequently established to ensure coordination and coherence in process, planning and scheduling and the exploitation of inter-programme complementarities. Participating agencies are the HEA, SFI, the HRB, EI, the IRCSET and the IRCHSS.

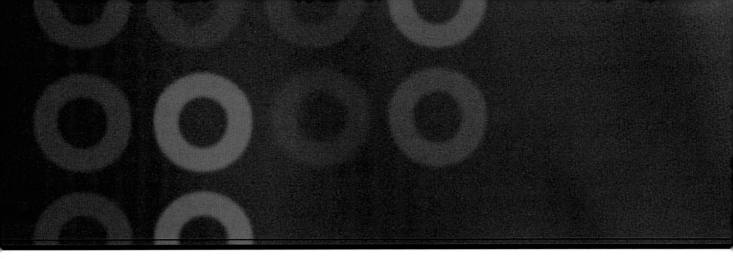

Key area for action

Fostering the disciplines of strategic management and associated organisational change and capacity building among the institutions that comprise the sector.

Developing and embedding as appropriate - comprehensive systems of evaluation which provides the basis of good governance and accountability; the stimulus to innovative, progressive action to enhance quality and breadth of provision to diverse participants; the means for benchmarking against international standards.

Key Tasks

Review of university strategies

The Universities Act, 1997 provides that the HEA may review the strategies of the universities as a means to assist them in their ongoing development and implementation of strategic plans. The HEA will institute and complete a process of review of strategic plans of the universities by end 2004.

Evaluate impact of targeted initiatives

The HEA undertakes regular evaluations of the targeted initiatives programmes which support institutional action in a range of identified national priorities. The HEA intends to continue these evaluations to assess the impact of existing funding, and to assist in both the mainstreaming of good practice and in the development of future targeted initiatives. Evaluations of the progression initiative, the Irish initiative and the access initiative are planned for 2004.

Key Outputs 2004 - 2007
Fostering strategic management, organisational change and capacity building

1. Report: *University Strategic Plans* (2004)

2. Report: Review of Targeted Initiatives [ongoing; progression (2004); Irish (2004); access (2004)]

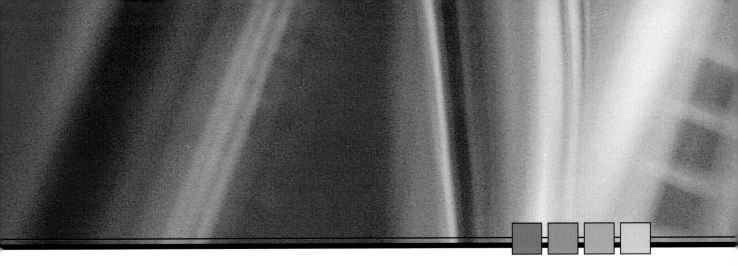

(2) Widening participation in higher education

> *Key area for action:*
> *Promote equity of access and opportunity in higher education.*

Key Tasks

Publish the report of Equality Review Team to the Higher Education Authority and support the institutions in the implementation of its recommendations

The HEA has a statutory function, under the Universities Act, 1997, to review university equality policies, thereby assisting the universities in developing their strategies and programmes to ensure equality of opportunity for both students and staff. In 2003 the HEA appointed a high level group to review university policies and to report to the Authority on their findings. This report will be published in spring 2004 and its recommendations implemented during 2004-5.

Survey of higher education entrants

During 2003 the HEA commissioned a further survey of higher education entrants, to report in early 2004. This survey will continue the series of reports commissioned by the HEA since 1980 to examine the profile of new entrants to higher education.

During 2004-2007 a full national survey of all new entrants to higher education in the relevant year will take place.

National plan to support equity of access to higher education

Following a decision by the Minister for Education and Science, the National Office for Equity of Access to Higher Education ('National Office') was established in the HEA in August 2003. The remit of the National Office is to facilitate inclusive and equitable access to higher education by under-represented groups, in particular those who are socially or economically disadvantaged, mature learners and those with a disability.

In 2004 the National Office will publish a national multi-annual plan to achieve equity of access to higher education. The plan will be developed in consultation with learners, education partners, social partners and other stakeholders. The plan will be implemented during 2005-7.

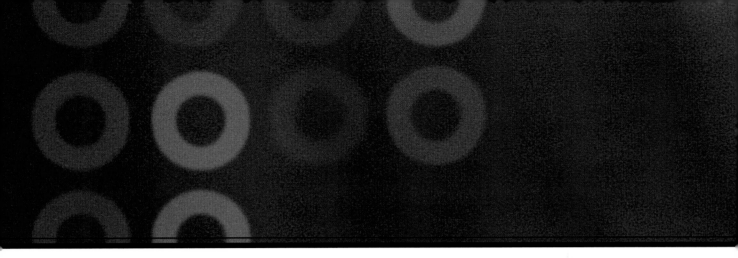

Allocate funding to facilitate equity of access to higher education

From early 2004 the National Office will manage allocation of funding to support wider participation in higher education. Programmes include the Targeted Initiative Scheme to Improve Access, the Special Fund for Students with Disabilities, the Student Assistance Fund and the Millennium Partnership Fund.

Review of funding programmes that promote wider participation in higher education

During 2004 the National Office will conduct a review of funding programmes and publish recommendations for consolidation and future policy development

---

Key Outputs 2004 - 2007
Promote equity of access and opportunity in higher education

1. Report: *Report of Equality Review Team to the Higher Education Authority* (2004) and implementation of recommendations (2004 - 2005)

2. Report: *Sample Survey of Higher Education Entrants* (2004);
   Report: *National Survey of Higher Education Entrants* (2005)

3. Publication of national plan to achieve equity of access to higher education by the National Office for Equity of Access to Higher Education (2004)

4. Implementation of national strategy to achieve equity of access (2005-2007)

5. Review of Targeted Initiative Scheme to Improve Access (2004)

6. Allocation of funding to facilitate equity of access to higher education (on-going)

7. Publication of review of funding programmes that promote wider participation in higher education (2004)

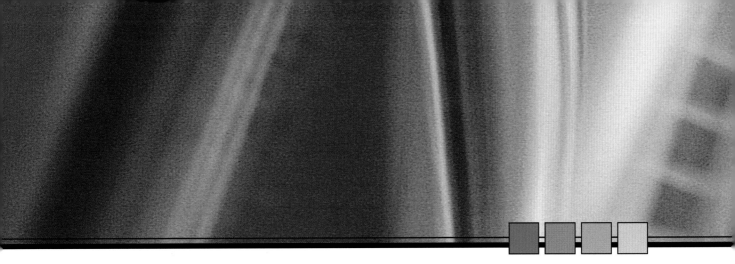

Key area for action

Promote successful participation in higher education.

Key Tasks

Identify factors associated with non-completion

Following the publication of the report on the levels of non-completion in the university sector in 2001, the HEA will work with the higher education institutions to review the qualitative factors associated with non-completion of courses and identify ways of tackling the problem.

Enhance the student records system

The HEA has been requested by the Department of Education and Science to develop and manage a new and comprehensive student record system that will capture information about students in all higher education institutions. The first of its type in Irish higher education, this database will provide comprehensive data on variables associated with student participation in higher education, and will support better analysis of student participation and completion in higher education. During 2004 a working party will be established to develop the new system. The database is due to be operational in all HEA institutions by the end of 2004 and will be extended on a phased basis to the institutes of technology.

Review student retention policies

The HEA will review institutional student retention policies and identify models of best practice that will support the institutions in the further development of policy and in the allocation of funding. This review will take place in 2004.

Support targeted initiative funding for measures to support student completion

The HEA will continue to provide financial support to the institutions in their programmes to enhance student completion of courses in higher education.

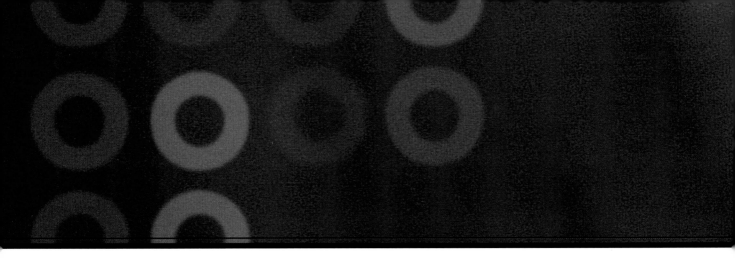

1. Working with the HEIs to review qualitative factors associated with non-completion of courses and identification of ways to address the problem (2004)

2. Development and implementation of new higher education student record system (2004-2005)

3. Publication of Report on Student Completion Policies in Higher Education Institutions (2004)

4. Allocation of funding to institutions to support successful participation policies (2004-2007)

Key area for action
Foster links that facilitate student movement and progression within the education system as a whole.

Key Tasks

Facilitate enhanced opportunities to access higher education

The National Office for Equity of Access to Higher Education will, in co-operation with the Department of Education and Science, NQAI, HETAC and FETAC support the creation of new pathways for progression between further and higher education and within higher education.

Support development of policies and practices in institutions to develop a common European area of higher education

Through the Bologna process, the Ministers for Education of thirty-seven European countries including Ireland have committed to support the development of a common European area of higher education, including movement towards mutual recognition of awards. The HEA is working with the Department of Education and Science and other relevant stakeholders to support this process.

Evaluation of the targeted initiative to support progression

We have already noted the various evaluations of targeted initiatives that will take place over the course of this strategy. Of particular relevance to this key area for action is the progression initiative. This initiative will be evaluated in 2004.

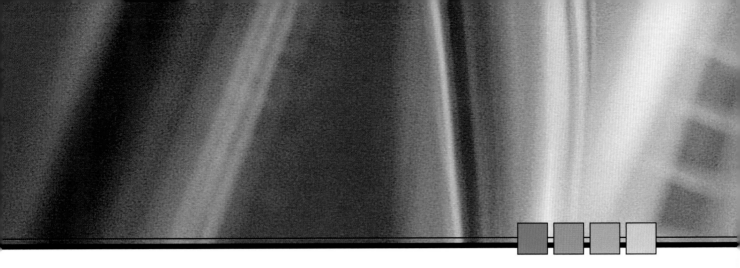

Key Outputs
Foster links that facilitate student movement and progression within the education system as a whole

1. Consultation underway on progression routes from further to higher education and within higher education (2004)

2. Bologna process implemented within education system in Ireland (on-going)

3. Review of the Progression Targeted Initiative (2004)

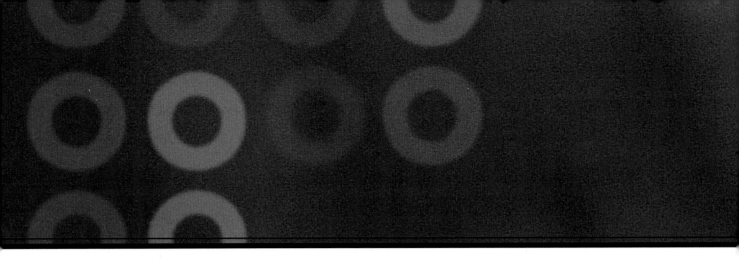

(3) Fostering the development of a higher education sector which has the capacity to respond to changing needs in society

---

Key areas for action:

Advise the Minister for Education and Science and Government on all matters pertaining to higher education and assure Government and the general public as to the effectiveness and efficiency of the system.

Develop policies and procedures to ensure that the Irish system is appropriately linked to European and wider international systems of higher education.

Monitor developments on a global stage and locally that are relevant to higher education in Ireland.

Contribute and support other agencies/bodies in the development of policy.

Key Tasks

Provision of support to the institutions in attracting required resources

In the more competitive, global environment for higher education, institutions are increasingly having regard to the need to attract both staff and students. The HEA has recently published reports designed to assist (1) the institutions in the attraction and retention of researchers from abroad, and (2) on a new framework to attract overseas students to enter Irish higher education. Arising from these reports the HEA will work with the institutions, and also the Department of Education and Science and other stakeholders in addressing these issues.

Designation of Institutes of Technology

The Minister for Education and Science has proposed to transfer responsibility for funding the institutes of technology from the Department of Education and Science to the HEA[10]. This will require both legislative and operational changes. The HEA will work with the Department of Education and Science and institutes to prepare for this change. Since the creation of the technological sector, the institutes have developed to play a critical part in meeting the economic, social and cultural needs of their regions and nationally. The HEA looks forward to supporting the institutes as they continue to play this role into the future.

---

10 Initiation of this transfer is pending the report of the OECD review of higher education in Ireland.

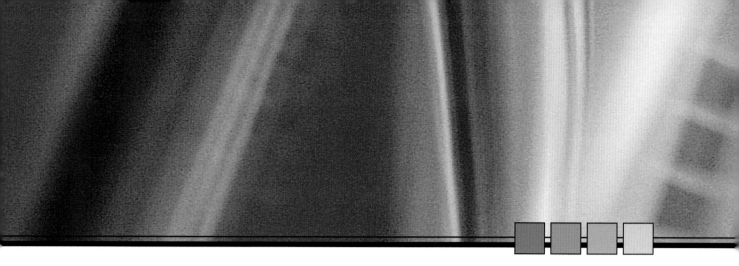

HEA submission to the OECD review team

The OECD is carrying out a review of higher education in Ireland in 2004. The HEA was asked to make a submission to the review team covering all aspects of higher education. This submission was submitted to the review team in January 2004. In particular, the Authority set out its view of the essential contribution that the higher education institutions make to both students and to society as a whole in social, economic and cultural terms. The Authority considers that the most effective means to support this contribution is through a governance framework that balances institutional autonomy with appropriate accountability. The Authority looks forward to the outcome of the OECD review and developing its strategy arising from Government decisions and actions in response to the review's recommendations.

Review of mature student participation

The HEA is currently considering the position of mature students participation in Irish higher education, particularly to assess the numbers and characteristics of adults who have not benefited from access to higher education. The research, which will be completed in summer 2004, will support measures to enhance mature student participation into the future.

Euro Student survey

A second Euro Student survey will take place in 2004. This survey aims to deliver fundamental information on the social and economic conditions of student life in Europe and to condense this information into the form of comparable indicators. This study will better inform the HEA and other stakeholders in Ireland on trends in student participation in Ireland measured within a European context. In the light of the importance of increasing student mobility across member states it is important that Ireland contributes to, and participates fully, in this survey.

Statistics

The advisory function will continue to be supported by the range of statistical publications produced on an annual basis by the HEA, e.g. First Destination Report, Annual Statistics Report on Student Flows. The publications also support the work of a variety of stakeholders.

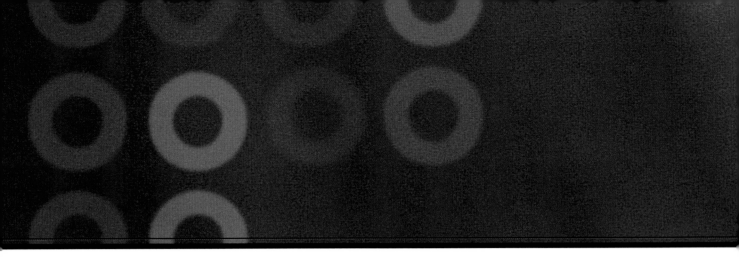

Provision of advice to other agencies/bodies

The HEA will continue to contribute to, and support, the work of other agencies/bodies in the development of policy. A critical element of the HEA's work is the support and advice that it provides to bodies including most recently the Expert Group on Future Skills Needs, the National Adult Learning Council, the Enterprise Strategy Group, the Task Force on Medical Education, etc. The HEA regards this work as critically important to its activities and will continue to assist these bodies and other bodies, as required.

Key Outputs 2004 - 2007
Fostering the development of a higher education sector which has the capacity to respond to changing needs in society

1. Supporting HEIs in attracting required resources (on-going)

2. Designation of institutes of technology (after OECD review)

3. Submission to the OECD review team (2004)

4. Report: Review of Mature Student Participation (2004)

5. Euro Student Survey (2004)

6. Statistical reports (on-going)

7. Provision of advice to other agencies/bodies (on-going)

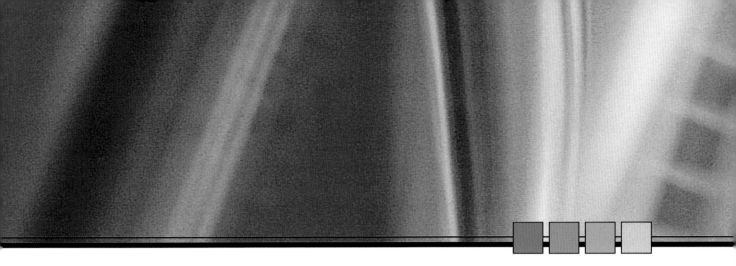

(4) Strengthening HEA Capability

> *Key areas for action:*
>
> *Maintain appropriate resources and skill sets to meet expanding needs.*
>
> *Introduce and continually upgrade quality and performance management systems.*
>
> *Invest and upgrade the physical resources, (premises, IT systems) required to carry out organisational functions and objectives.*

Key Tasks

Ensuring appropriate staff numbers and skills and competencies to meet expanding needs

The most critical resource available to the HEA to deliver on the vision and priorities set out in this strategy statement are its people. The HEA is committed to the continuing development of our staff and providing opportunities to assist in developing and strengthening skills and competencies. In the context of the HEA's expanding remit, staff numbers will be reviewed to ensure that the size of the people resource is sufficient to meet the organisation's demands.

HEA internal audit

The HEA undertook a systematic evaluation of risk management within the organisation. Work is underway regarding the implementation of recommendations arising from this process. The HEA, with the assistance of its internal auditors, will continue to review critical risk areas, and to develop appropriate policies and procedures to safeguard against those risks.

Introduction of Performance Management and Development System

The HEA is developing a performance management and development system (PMDS) in consultation with staff. It will provide a structured and planned approach to staff development and performance management. The introduction of PMDS will facilitate staff development needs and the maintenance/development of appropriate skills and competencies to meet the expanding work of the HEA.

Development of new Information Technology (IT) systems

The HEA will match its IT capabilities to changing needs and will upgrade a number of key systems in 2004 to ensure optimum performance.

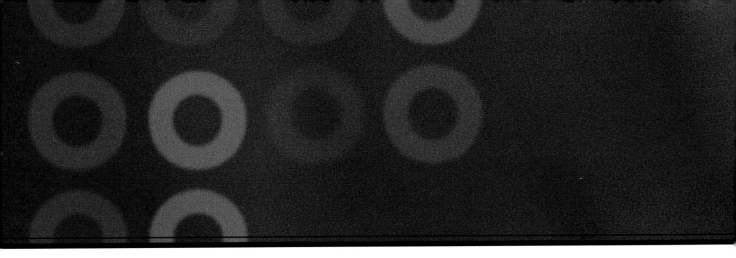

Development of quality customer service plan

As the HEA's functional responsibilities expand it will seek to improve its standards of service. This will involve focusing on the needs of recipients, the setting of challenging standards in service delivery and making the best use of available resources. The HEA will assess how best to ensure that it is carrying out its functions in an effective and responsive manner, this will include examining the introduction of an appropriate system of quality assurance in 2004.

Planning to meet requirements under the Official Languages Act

It is anticipated that the HEA will be named as a designated organisation under the Official Languages Act. Following from this designation the HEA will be required to prepare a plan for meeting its requirements under the Act and will be allocated 3 years to deliver on its commitments. Preparations are already underway in this respect, e.g. the upgrading of the website includes an Irish translation of the site, a number of staff have attended relevant training courses.

Key Outputs 2004 - 2007
Strengthening HEA capability

1. Ensuring appropriate staff numbers, skills and competencies (on-going)

2. Internal Audit: Implementation of the recommendations of this risk management review
   (2004 with on-going review of critical risk areas)

3. Implementation of Performance Management and Development System (2004)

4. Upgrading of First Destination Report database, unit cost database and the HEA website (2004)

5. Development of customer service plan (2004)

6. Planning for, and delivery of service, in accordance with our requirements under the Official Languages Act
   (2004 - 2007)

chapter four | Implementing the Strategic Plan

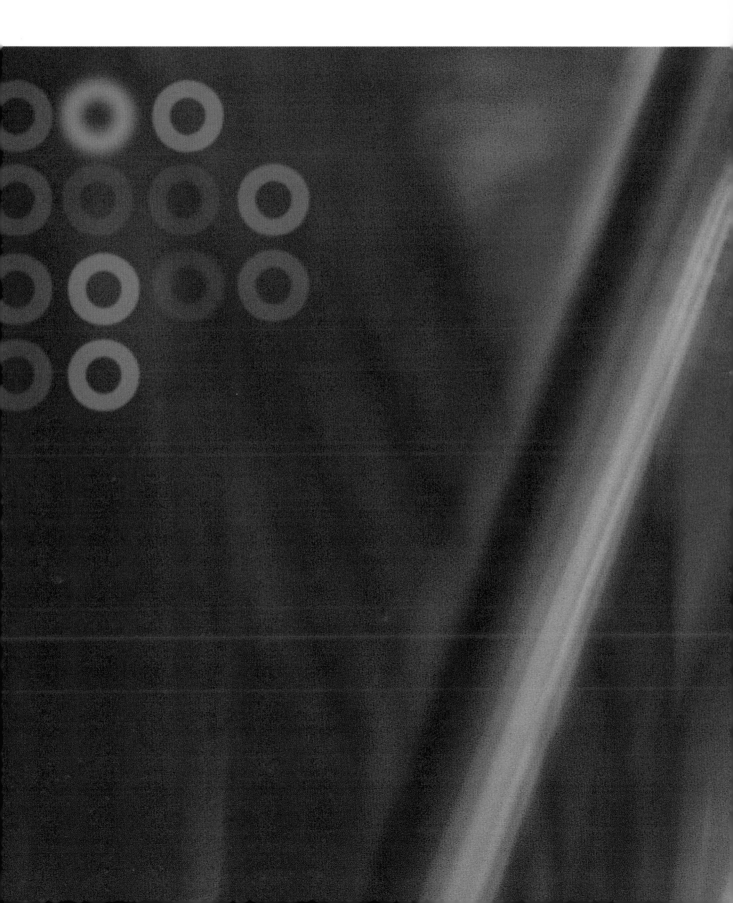

4. Implementing the Strategic Plan

Progress and Evaluation

An annual work plan will set out tasks to progress the implementation of the strategy as well as delivery dates. This will enable the Authority to review progress and to identify and address variations from the plan. Outcomes and progress will be addressed in the annual report. A formal implementation review will take place annually to assess progress in meeting defined goals and time frames but also stakeholder views and external evaluations. This will check progress as well as identifying priorities for the following year.

Organisation and Resources

Structures and capacity will be monitored on a continuing basis. The Authority will work to ensure that the HEA organisation has the appropriate resources to implement the strategic plan and to perform its core functions of:

- resource allocation
- policy evaluation
- review, analysis and advice on the development of the higher education sector.

appendices

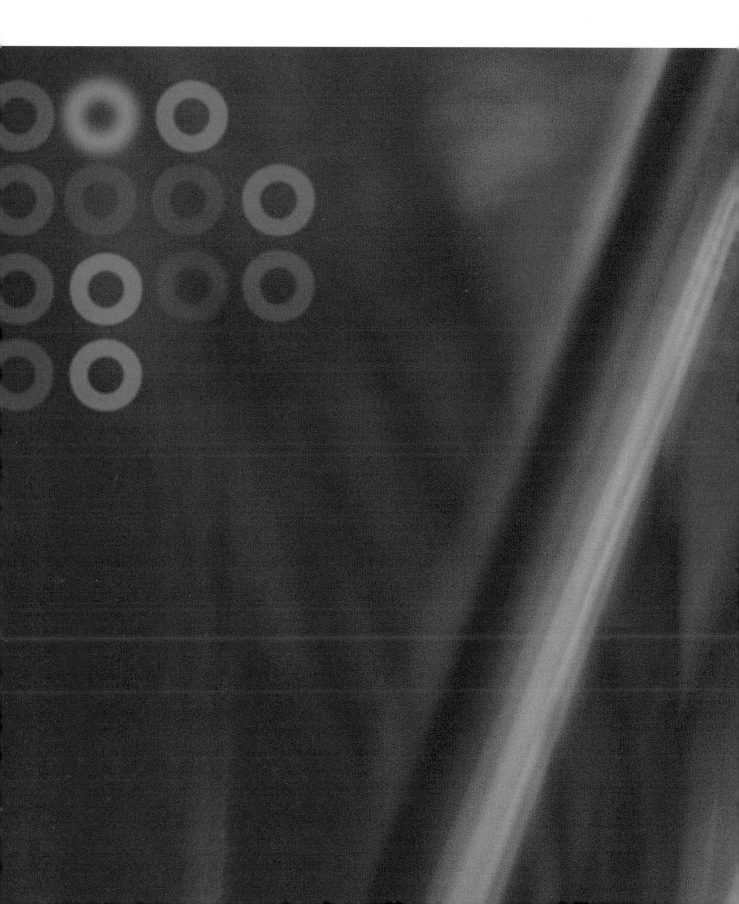

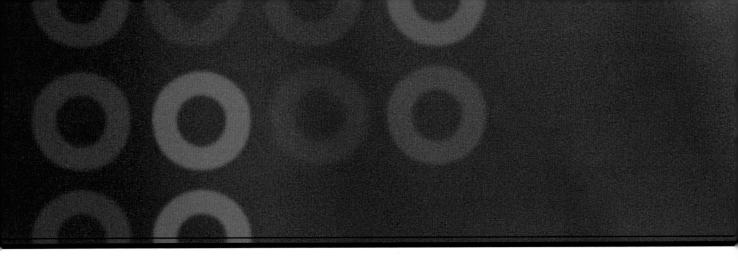

Appendix 1

Implementation Timetable

The following implementation timetable sets out the expected completion dates for the key outputs identified in this strategy statement. These are not a full list of outputs that will be completed in 2004 - 2007; they are indicative of the work programme for 2004/early 2005. Additional tasks required to further the achievement of our strategic priorities will become evident over the lifetime of the strategy. Our work programme for 2004 also involves a significant amount of policy review and formulation work. This will contribute to informing implementation and further policy review work that will follow in 2005 - 2007.

Key Tasks	Expected Completion Timeframes for Key Outputs						
	Q1 2004	Q2 2004	Q3 2004	Q4 2004	2005	2006	2007
(1) Empowering Institutions							
Report on quality assurance				▓			
Review of recurrent funding model – consultation paper and consultation process	▓	▓					
Report on capital projects prioritisation		▓					
Development of new model for capital project mgt.		▓	▓				
Funding framework to support skills needs	▓	▓	▓	▓	▓	▓	▓
PRTLI Impact Assessment		▓					
Determine strategic direction of PRTLI & input into next NDP					▓	▓	
PRTLI Cycle 4 (call for proposals and allocations)				▓	▓		
Attracting and retaining researchers	▓	▓	▓	▓	▓	▓	▓
Supporting HEIs in relation to the European Research Area	▓	▓	▓	▓	▓	▓	▓
Support the management of research funding – Merrion Group	▓	▓	▓	▓	▓	▓	▓
Review of university strategic plans (according to S.49 Universities Act)				▓			
Review of Targeted Initiatives	▓	▓	▓	▓	▓	▓	▓
Review of progression, Irish and access initiatives				▓			

Key Tasks	Expected Completion Timeframes for Key Outputs						
	Q1 2004	Q2 2004	Q3 2004	Q4 2004	2005	2006	2007
(2) Widening Participation in Higher Education							
Report of the Equality Review Group	■	■					
Survey of 2003 higher education entrants		■					
Full national survey of higher education entrants					■		
Launch of national plan for achieving equity of access				■			
Allocation of funding to achieve equity of access	▒	▒	▒	▒	▒	▒	▒
Review of access related funding programmes		■	■	■			
Tackling barriers to successful completion	▒	▒	▒	▒	▒	▒	▒
Enhance student records system				■			
Review student retention policies				■			
Support completion through targeted initiative	▒	▒	▒	▒	▒	▒	▒
Facilitate enhanced opportunities to access	▒	▒	▒	▒	▒	▒	▒
Support development of a common European area of higher education	▒	▒	▒	▒	▒	▒	▒
(3) Fostering the development of a higher education sector which has the capacity to respond to changing needs in society							
Support the HEIs in attracting required resources	▒	▒	▒	▒	▒	▒	▒
Designation of ITs under the HEA (expected by end 2004)				■			
Preparation of submission to OECD review team	■						
Review of mature student participation		■					
Euro student survey				■			
Statistical reports	▒	▒	▒	▒	▒	▒	▒
Advice to agencies/bodies	▒	▒	▒	▒	▒	▒	▒
(4) Strengthening HEA capability							
Ensuring staff numbers, skills and competencies	▒	▒	▒	▒	▒	▒	▒
Ongoing review of critical risk areas	▒	▒	▒	▒	▒	▒	▒
Introduction of PMDS	■	■	■				
Upgrading of selected IT systems				■			
Launch of customer service plan				■			
Meeting requirements of Official Languages Act	▒	▒	▒	▒	▒	▒	▒

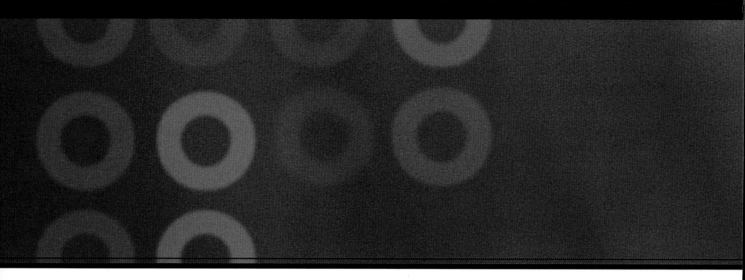

Appendix 2

Overview of National Research System

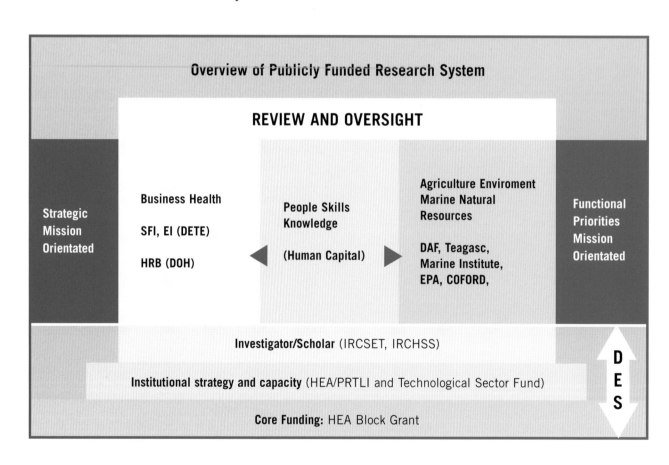

Overview of Publicly Funded Research System

REVIEW AND OVERSIGHT

| Strategic Mission Orientated | Business Health SFI, EI (DETE) HRB (DOH) | People Skills Knowledge (Human Capital) | Agriculture Enviroment Marine Natural Resources DAF, Teagasc, Marine Institute, EPA, COFORD, | Functional Priorities Mission Orientated |

Investigator/Scholar (IRCSET, IRCHSS)

Institutional strategy and capacity (HEA/PRTLI and Technological Sector Fund)

Core Funding: HEA Block Grant

D
E
S

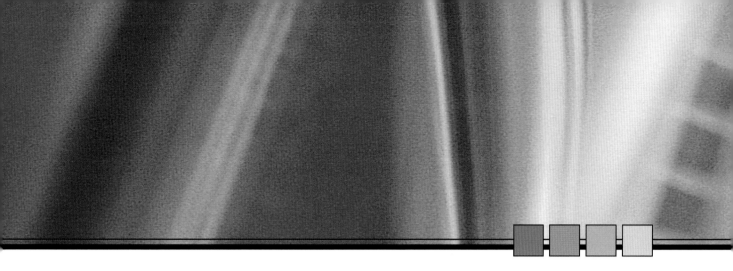

Appendix 3

HEA – Some key contributions to Irish higher education

This section reviews some of the work of the Authority in shaping the development of the higher education sector, in recent years, particularly as it relates to the strategic objectives set out in this strategy statement.

(1) Empowering the institutions

The HEA has a major role in supporting the quality of Ireland's higher education institutions. There has been a transformation in the physical infrastructure of the sector which is obvious to all; but this has been matched by increased attention to the management of institutions and the sector and the quality of teaching and research it affords to the nation. The publication with the Conference of Heads of Irish Universities of *The University Challenged (Malcolm Skilbeck, 2001)* identified major issues to be addressed in higher education provision.

In the area of research there has been particularly exciting progress. The HEA has since 1998 managed the allocation of unprecedented levels of research funding to the higher education sector – some €600 million to date. The funding is allocated on a competitive basis, assessing institutional strategy, the quality of research proposal, the link with teaching and learning, and collaboration with other institutions. It has acted as a catalyst in encouraging institutions critically to asses their research strategies and to adopt a strategy approach to their institution's research plans. To date, PRTLI funding has resulted in 62 new and expanded research programmes, a 280% increase in research space funded and almost 800 new post-graduate research posts. The impact is demonstrated in the 1,900 publications arising from PRTLI funded programme – a 250% increase in output over the previous period. This is a quantum leap in Irish research and the impact it can make internationally.

The HEA provides funding to the institutions in a number of ways. Most importantly, the HEA provides block grants to each university annually for their teaching and research activities, based on a unit cost model.

The HEA also operates the Targeted Initiative Scheme to support institutions to develop and implement programmes to address national priorities, such as access, support for teaching, retention and progression. Funding is allocated on a competitive basis, including criteria such as the quality of proposal, level of co-funding proposed, and link with institutional strategy. The Training of Trainers Scheme funds the development of training capability within the institution through the training of trainers, rather than direct provision. Key areas that have benefited are

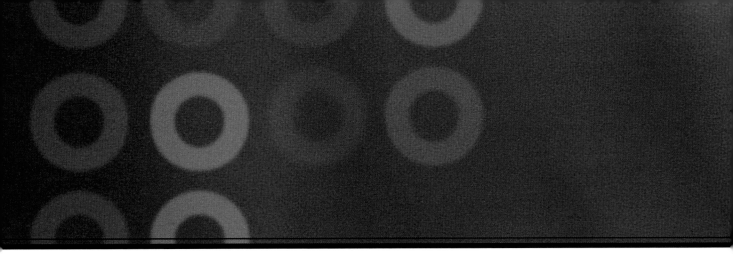

management of pedagogical (teaching) practice, and freedom of information. The Quality Assurance/Improvement programmes supports the institutions in their development of quality assurance procedures.

The HEA also supports extra provision to meet identified skills shortages, for example, in healthcare, ICT and pharmacy through dedicated competitive funding.

Finally, the HEA also supports the capital programmes of the universities through both the provision of dedicated funding for individual projects, and through other initiatives such as a major building condition survey, a maintenance work programme, a regular space inventory survey and the commencement of a survey of research equipment.

(2) Widening participation in higher education

Higher Education has a critical role in modern society. Through the development, and dissemination of knowledge and skills, the higher education sector underpins national development, in economic, social and cultural terms.

The higher education sector also supports individuals. Access to and participation in higher education provides the opportunities for individuals to explore and achieve their potential. In purely economic terms, this is important; evidence internationally consistently demonstrates that individuals who have participated in higher education benefit from higher returns compared with those who have not.

Yet at a more fundamental level, participation in higher education can also be seen as a critical contributor to the development of citizenship. Prof. Malcolm Skilbeck in his report to the HEA "Meeting the Equity Challenge in Higher Education" (1999) noted "Equity is sometimes subsumed under the concept of democratisation: all individuals have rights and needs, which must feature in education in policies and action strategies. Through participative procedures, all can have a voice and an impact."

In Ireland there has been significant progress in broadening access to higher education. For example, the transfer rate from second to third level has increased from 11% in 1965, to almost 57% today.*

---

* The rate of transfer is estimated by taking total annual intake to all third level colleges as a percentage of the estimated population at age 17. Some persons entering third level may have previously entered. Mature Students and entrants from outside the state are also included.

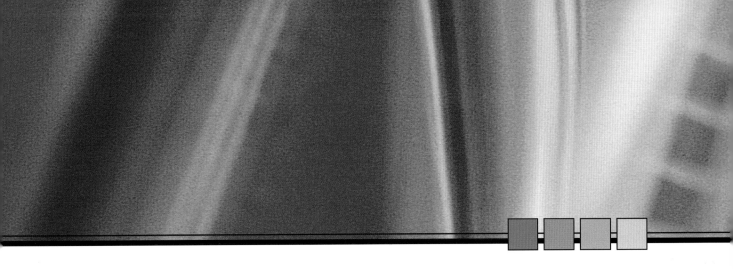

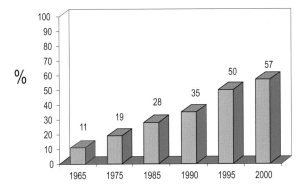

Such a rate compares favourably with other OECD countries, for example the target rate for access to higher education in England and Wales is for 50% of all 18-30 year olds to access higher education – a target we have already surpassed.

However, more remains to be done. A crucial area is that of access by socio-economically disadvantaged students to higher education. The surveys by Clancy carried out for the HEA show that while real progress has been made since 1980, lower socio-economic groups remain badly under-represented in higher education.

Estimate Proportion of Age Cohort Entering Full-Time Higher Education by Fathers' Socio-Economic Group in 1980, 1986, 1992 and 1998

Socio-Economic Groups	1998	1992	1986	1980
Farmers	0.75	0.53	0.42	0.30
Other Agricultural Occupations	0.35	0.24	0.12	0.06
Higher Professional	1.00*	0.85	0.72	0.59
Lower Professional	0.48	0.42	0.47	0.33
Employers and Managers	0.84	0.67	0.45	0.42
Salaried Employers	0.55	0.48	0.58	0.59
Intermediate Non-Manual Workers	0.33	0.27	0.28	0.22
Other Non-Manual Workers	0.31	0.26	0.11	0.09
Skilled Manual Workers	0.34	0.28	0.13	0.09
Semi-Skilled Manual	0.23	0.19	0.11	0.09
Unskilled Manual Workers	0.22	0.12	0.04	0.03
Total	**0.46**	**0.36**	**0.25**	**0.20**

* This is an overestimate

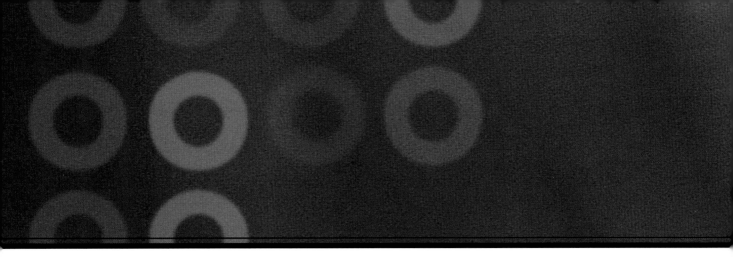

The primary actors in this challenge are the higher education institutions. Both the institutes in the technological sector and the universities have statutory objectives to support increased equality of access to higher education; the universities being specifically required to prepare and implement targeted policies. The HEA has recently undertaken a review of these policies and this report will be published shortly.

The Skilbeck report highlighted above reviewed international strategies to enhance access and participation and provided a series of recommendations for the institutions, the HEA and other stakeholders to support such enhanced participation.

A further key measure of access and participation is the proportion of students who complete their course. A HEA review of non-completion undertaken by Dr. Mark Morgan in 2001 showed that 83% of university students complete their course; ranking Ireland second among OECD countries at that time. This figure does however conceal certain weaknesses, particularly in key disciplines such as ICT. Non-completion of courses is costly to the institutions and the state and can prove a very negative personal experience for students.

Drawing on the work and recommendations of Skilbeck, Morgan and others, the HEA has sought to support the institutions in addressing the challenge of enhancing access and participation. The HEA has provided specific funding, through the targeted initiatives scheme, to support the institutions to broaden access to higher education. Since 1996 funding of over €25 million has been provided to the universities and HEA-designated institutions to improve access for a range of under-represented groups, including school-leavers from disadvantaged backgrounds, mature students and students with disabilities, and travellers and refugees. Since 1999 €2 million has been provided to the universities and HEA-designated institutions to support students that may be at risk of non-completion. Initiatives undertaken by the institutions include courses in foundation subjects such as mathematics and extra tutorial support in subjects with higher non-completion rates.

Through the commissioning and publication of key research, and the provision of targeted initiative funding, the HEA has sought to provide support to the institutions in their mission to enhance access to and participation in higher education. The challenge for the future will be for the institutions to continue and intensify the work already being done to broaden access. This will be achieved through the development of collaborative approaches within and indeed beyond higher education to create new pathways and opportunities for students to access higher education,

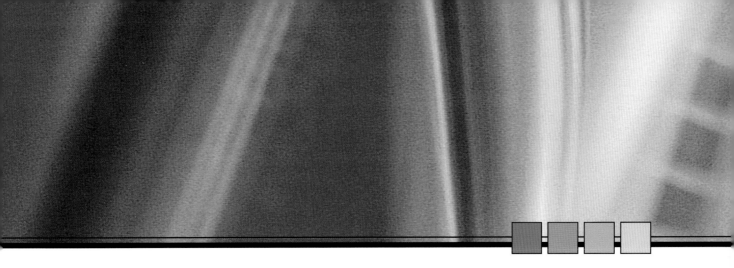

and, upon entry, to appropriately support those students in successful participation in higher education. The HEA will continue to support the institutions in this challenge, through research, advice and funding.

(3) Fostering the development of a higher education sector which has the capacity to respond to changing needs in society

The activities and programmes outlined above are all generated by the HEA's policy advice development role which identifies areas for action and informs strategies to be followed. By means of example the following paragraphs provide a snapshot of some areas of the HEA's policy advice.

The PRTLI grew from a recognition of the need to support Irish research in order to achieve a society and economy founded on innovation. The design, development and management of the programme on behalf of the Minister for Education and Science were the next steps from the policy formulation. The report, *Creating and Sustaining an Innovation Society (2002)*, outlines the shift in public policy which is necessary to move Ireland from a situation where economic growth relies on foreign direct investment and imported technology to one where the basis for growth arises from indigenous innovation. This policy has been further developed in *Creating Ireland's Innovation Society: The Next Strategic Step (2003)* which looks at attracting and retaining researchers in Ireland.

The work of the HEA also feeds into broader national education policies. As part of its policy advice role, the HEA has both undertaken and supported a number of major policy reports on the development of higher education in Ireland such as the report of the *Steering Group on Higher Education (1995) and the Report on the Post-Secondary Education and Training (1999).* This was the report of a working group set up to advise on the appropriate level of provision of education and training places for school leavers and others, e.g. mature students.

Likewise, the HEA has played a major role in the development of a national policy to improve access to higher education – through policy advice, participation on the Action Group on Access to Third Level Education as well as targeted funding. In the context of this work, HEA research and commissioned research is drawn upon as important information sources, for example, the report *College Entry in Focus: A Fourth National Survey of Access to Higher Education (2001) (Patrick Clancy)* presents the findings of a study that examined the pattern of participation in higher education in Ireland. It was based on a national survey of all those who enrolled as new entrants to full-time

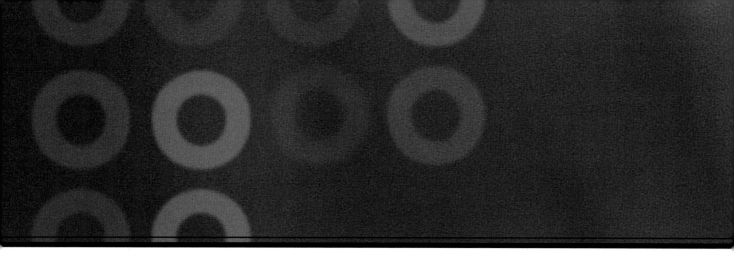

higher education in Autumn 1998. The findings were of particular interest in terms of identifying trends in the socio-economic backgrounds of entrants to higher education.

In the HEA/CHIU commissioned report – *The University Challenged* by Malcolm Skilbeck (2001) - the extensive demands that are being placed on higher education institutions by Government, industry, social partners, parents, students, professional bodies and other interested parties were examined. Existing performances were assessed and recommendations were made on strategies to ensure that the higher education system is equipped to deal with the new and emerging challenges.

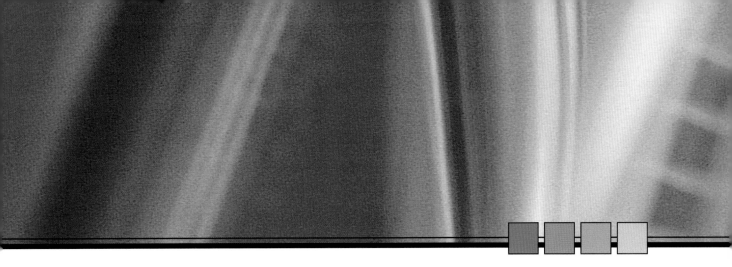

Appendix 4

List of Parties Consulted

CHIU

Council of Directors

Department of Education & Science

Department of Enterprise,
Trade & Employment

Enterprise Ireland

FÁS

FETAC

Forfás

Health Research Board

HETAC

IBEC

ICTU

IDA

IRCHSS

IRCSET

NQAI

Science Foundation Ireland

USI

List of Acronyms Used

CHIU	Conference of Heads of Irish Universities
DES	Department of Education and Science
DETE	Department of Enterprise, Trade and Employment
EI	Enterprise Ireland
ERA	European Research Area
FETAC	Further Education and Training Awards Council
HEA	Higher Education Authority
HEI	Higher Education Institution
HETAC	Higher Education and Training Awards Council
HRB	Health Research Board
IBEC	Irish Business and Employers Confederation
ICTU	Irish Congress of Trade Unions
IDA	Industrial Development Authority
IRCHSS	Irish Research Council for the Humanities and Social Sciences
IRCSET	Irish Research Council for Science, Engineering and Technology
IUQB	Irish Universities Quality Board
IT	Institute of Technology
NQAI	National Qualifications Authority of Ireland
OECD	Organisation for Economic Co-operation and Development
PMDS	Performance Management Development System
PRTLI	Programme for Research in Third Level Institutions
SFI	Science Foundation Ireland
USI	Union of Students in Ireland

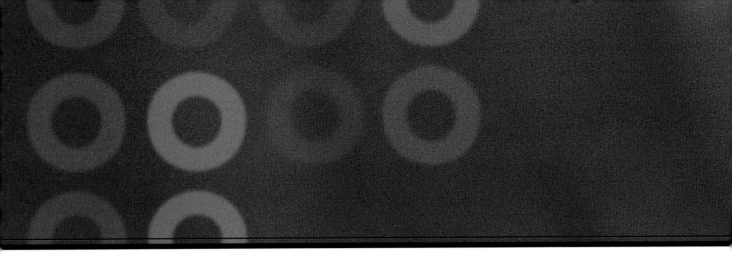

Appendix 5

Key Publications by HEA

- Creating Ireland's Knowledge Society: Proposals for Higher Education Reform -
  A Submission by the HEA to the OECD Review of Higher Education in Ireland (2004)

- The PRTLI Transforming the Irish Research in Education Landscape (2003)

- Provision of Undergraduate and Taught Postgraduate Education to Overseas Students in Ireland (2003)

- Report of the Group on Research Overheads (2003)

- Creating Ireland's Innovation Society: The Next Strategic Step – Professor Liam Downey (2003)

- Reports, Accounts 1997 & 1998. Student Statistics 1996/97 & 1997/98 (2002)

- Creating and Sustaining the Innovation Society (2002)

- Euro Student Social and Economic Conditions of Student Life in Europe 2000 - (HIS) (2002)

- First Destination of Award Recipients in Higher Education (2000): A Composite Report (2002)

- College Entry in Focus: A Fourth National Survey of Access to Higher Education –
  Professor Patrick Clancy (2001)

- The Financial Governance of Irish Universities - Balancing Autonomy and Accountability (2001)

- Euro Student Survey 2000: Irish Report - Social and Living Conditions of Higher Education Students -
  Professor Liam Ryan and Ms Caroline O'Kelly (2001)

- The University Challenged - A Review of International Trends and Issues with Particular Reference to Ireland –
  Professor Malcolm Skilbeck (2001)

- Programme for Research in Third Level Institutions - Information Guide 2001

- First Destination of Award Recipients in Higher Education (1999): A Composite Report (2001)

- A Study of Non-Completion in Undergraduate University Courses - by Dr. Mark Morgan, Ms Rita Flanagan and
  Dr. Thomas Kellaghan (Educational Research Centre) (2001)

- Social Background of Higher Education Entrants – Professor Patrick Clancy and Ms Joy Wall (2000)

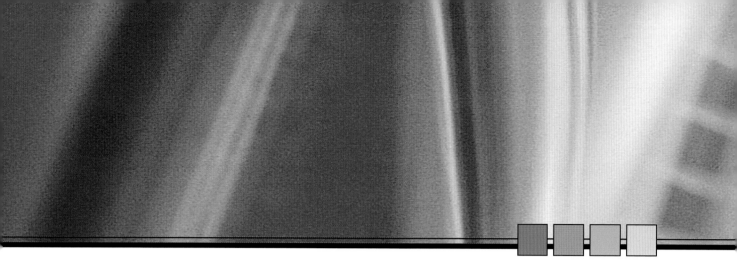

- Report to the Higher Education Authority on the Evaluation of the Targeted Initiative on Widening Access for Young People from Socio-Economically Disadvantaged Backgrounds. (2000)

- Forum on the Need for Pharmacy Graduates (2000)

- Report on Symposium on Open and Distance Learning (2000)

- Analysis of 1997/98 Student Application & Entry Data in and between the UK and Ireland (2000)

- Meeting the Equity Challenge in Higher Education: A Review of International Experience. [A Short version of Access and Equity in Higher Education An International Perspective on Issues and Strategies] by Professor Malcolm Skilbeck (2000)

- Access and Equity in Higher Education: An International Perspective on Issues and Strategies by Professor Malcolm Skilbeck (2000)

- First Destination of Award Recipients in Higher Education (1998): A composite Report (2000)

- The Humanities and the Social Sciences: A Case for a Research Council (1999)

- Technical Working group on the Review of Outreach Centres of Higher Education Institutions (1999)

- Assessing Supply in Relation to Prospective Demand for Pharmacists in Ireland (1999)

- Declining a Third Level Offer (Report by Professor Patrick Clancy) (1999)

- Report of Review Committee on Post Secondary Education and Training Places (1999)

- HEA Submission to Commission on the Points System (1999)

- Recommendation of the Higher Education Authority to government in accordance with the terms of Section 9 of the Universities Act, 1997 (1999)

- Review of the application by the Dublin Institute of Technology for establishment as a University under Section 9 of the Universities Act, 1997 (1998)

- A Comparative International Assessment of the Organisation, Management and funding of University research in Ireland and Europe Report of the CIRCA group Europe for the Higher Education Authority (1996).

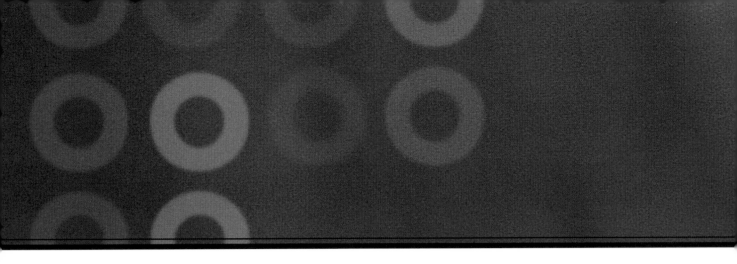

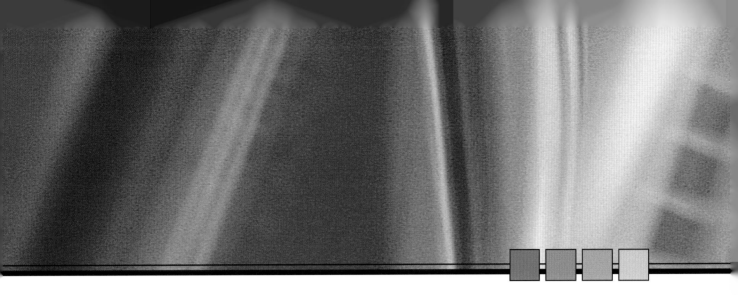